photographing

Paris

Amphoto
Travel
Guide

photographing
Paris

Albert Moldvay
Erika Fabian

Amphoto
American Photographic
Book Publishing Co., Inc.

NEW YORK, NEW YORK

Acknowledgements

Our thanks to Pan American World Airways, Agfa Gevaert, Vivitar, the French Government Tourist Office, and personally to Jerry and Colette for their help and cooperation.

All photographs by the authors
Design by The Graphic Image
Maps by John McAusland

Library of Congress Cataloging in Publication Data

Moldvay, Albert, 1921-
   Photographing Paris.

   (Amphoto travel guide)
   Includes index.
   1.   Travel photography.   2.   Paris.   I.   Fabian,
Erika, joint author.   II.   Title.
TR790.M65   778.9′9′944361083   79-26634

ISBN 0-8174-2124-6

Contents

Maps

ABOUT THE SYMBOLS

The numbered arrows on the maps are guides to show good locations for camera viewpoints. Symbols are used to rate the *visual importance* of each sight.

Three symbols mean that it is a *not-to-be-missed* picture.

Two symbols indicate that you should try for it but not at the expense of the "not-to-be-missed sights."

One symbol tells you, "this is another location that will make a good photograph."

One of the problems of photographing in a big city is that a sight is often missed simply because you didn't know it was there. We suggest that you follow the *Guide* and then return to other picture possibilities you may have seen along the way.

1. Things You Should Know About Paris

Paris is a city of vistas. Each landmark has an aesthetic viewpoint that seems to be made to order for photography. Most of the city streets have an "apartment-height" sameness, but the monotony is relieved by the mansard-roofed buildings full of chimneypots and the green trees, and colorful cafés and shops lining the sidewalks. The street intersections make good sites for photographs, because frequently the buildings stand at angles that make them look like huge stone ships pulling into harbor.

The Landmarks
The French have an exquisite sense of proportion and harmony. Each of the major landmarks has a view down a wide avenue, across a vast plaza, or over the waters of the Seine. It's as though each landmark were set in its own frame.

The Light
Often, the quality of the light makes a picture. You should be constantly aware of the sky. One minute it can be blazing blue and the next, gray or black; but most characteristic is an in-between luminescence that color-saturates your film. The familiar Parisian cityscape of wet, glowing cobblestoned streets reflecting the gaily colored dress of the passersby and the bright awnings of sidewalk cafés is not an unusual sight; you will have many chances to photograph such scenes from under your umbrella.

Other Sights
Besides the grand sights of Paris, there are many charming smaller ones that you can capture. The narrow crowded streets of MONTMARTRE, the cafés of the LATIN QUARTER, and the bookstalls along the Seine make happy picture-hunting grounds.

The People
The Parisians don't mind being photographed and are avid photographers themselves — after all, photography is a French invention. And they also think of photography more as art than as documentation. So added to the sights and the light is another necessary ingredient to good picture-taking: the bohemian spirit of Paris and the Parisians.

Sometimes the sky can be the most effective part of your composition. Emphasize it by tilting your camera upward to show more of the sky and less of the ground, as in this view of the Arc de Triomphe.

At Night

As a final capper, Paris has figured out that there are more hours in the day than daylight provides; the city glows for 24 hours, giving you many opportunities for illuminated night views and that mysterious mixture of daylight and incandescent light that drives color film mad.

A foreground statue can give ▶ depth and interest to a general view. Move around to compose your picture carefully. This Luxembourg Gardens shot would have looked silly with the statue pasted on the dome in back.

When shooting street candids, look for "typical" faces and attire to include in your scene—such as this couple in Montmartre.

THE BEST PICTURE TIME TO GO

When considering your trip to Paris, keep in mind that it is as far north as Newfoundland — just check your atlas. This means that the weather can be cool—in fact sometimes cold— even in summer. It also means that the light angle is lower, which is advantageous for pictures. Paris is also a wet place— an average of two days of rain per week—although sometimes the days add up to more than two. This may be uncomfortable for you but can be very good for pictures—just buy an umbrella and press on.

Spring
A favorite time for visiting Paris is in the Spring, when the chestnut trees are in bloom and the azaleas and flowering bulbs accent the fresh green of the grass and foliage.

Summer
The summer months of June and July are good for capturing the gay spirit of the outdoor cafés, the riverside philosophers by the SEINE, and the seemingly impromptu festivals, topped off by the big event—Bastille Day on July 14th.

If "you want to be alone," go to Paris in August, when all self-respecting Parisians are on holiday (unfortunately, so are many of the storekeepers). Then you can have the city to yourself without crowds.

Fall
Fall is visually more somber. By then, the proper European man has changed to his dark suit, and madame and mademoiselle to less revealing attire, but the weather usually remains pleasant throughout October.

Winter
The cold rains start in November, and from then until the first crocus peeps out, Paris is formal and indoors.

▲ Rain turns the Champs-Elysées into a mirror that reflects the colorful clothing of pedestrians.

Be prepared for the unexpected street shot by setting your shutter speed and f-stop ahead of time. When the right composition presents itself, just focus ▼ and shoot.

PICTURABLE FESTIVALS

Your first stop should be at the PARIS OFFICE OF TOURISM, which is at 127 CHAMPS-ELYSÉES, just down from the Arc de Triomphe on the left as you are facing the arch. There you can get up-to-the-minute information on current festivals and festivities that make good photos. But there are some that come around each year that you should know about.

March–October
A SOUND AND LIGHT SHOW at the INVALIDES — a chance for some night shooting (see "Tips and Techniques" section of this book).

May
PALM SUNDAY — a THRONE FAIR is held at VINCENNES (Reuilly Lawn).

May–September
The FOUNTAINS are turned on at VERSAILLES the first and third Sundays of the month from 4:30 to 6 P.M., and some nights they are floodlighted (Tel: 950-36-22, or check at the Paris Office of Tourism for times.) You will have to be on time for this event because there are many fountains to see (see "Tips and Techniques" for pointers).

June–July
MUSIC AND DRAMA FESTIVAL in the MARAIS QUARTER.

July 14
BASTILLE DAY FESTIVITIES — military marches, fireworks, and open-air celebrations. This is the best occasion to shoot a spectacle in Paris.

July–August
SUMMER FESTIVAL — takes place all over Paris, especially in the ILE DE LA CITÉ area along the Seine. (Check with the Tourist Department or the English-language papers as to where the festivities are held.)

October
WINE HARVEST FESTIVAL AT MONTMARTRE — a good time to shoot a bohemian activity in bohemian surroundings.

October–November
VETERAN CARS HILL RACE ON RUE LEPIC — another active event.

November 11
THE MILITARY PARADE DOWN THE CHAMPS-ELYSÉES from the Arc de Triomphe — a chance to get some colorful action if you missed the Bastille Day event.

December
CHRISTMAS ILLUMINATIONS ON THE CHAMPS-ELYSÉES — also a good time to see the churches.

▲ Contrasting detail, such as the ornate grilled gateway and the dome of the Commerce building on the Ile de la Cité, make an interesting study in design.

The kiosk, the umbrellas of a sidewalk café, and the typically Parisian buildings in the background make this street scene almost ▼ travel-poster perfect.

FRENCH CUSTOMS

The official French restriction on tourist photographers is 2 cameras of different types with 10 rolls of film or 24 plates, and/or 1 small motion picture camera with 10 rolls of film. (It says nothing about extra lenses and accessories.) There is an additional condition: The photographic equipment has to be re-exported (taken back with you).

In actual practice, on arrival you will stand in the line at Customs that says "Nothing to Declare"; or, if you have a considerable amount of equipment, you can leave a copy of the U.S. Customs registration and a deposit to guarantee that you will re-export the equipment that you brought in. The French bureaucracy is very accurate about filling out these forms. On previous trips to France we have listed our equipment, left a deposit, and were able to collect it upon leaving France.

RESTRICTIONS ON PHOTOGRAPHY

You will find that there are many restrictions on photography in Paris — not on the streets, but inside buildings and public places. Where they say no pictures are permitted, as inside the Comédie Française and the Opéra, they mean it and will enforce it. Where photography is permitted, such as in the Louvre, there is a fee attached and you will get a receipt. Keep the receipt; someone will want to see it.

SAFETY PRECAUTIONS

Be careful with your photographic equipment; don't leave it lying about, and watch it especially at night when taking pictures of the illuminated sights. Paris is a relatively safe place, but even there, notices are flashed on the theater screens warning you to hold your bag in your lap and not put it under your seat where it might be stolen.

It is safe to shoot at night along the boulevards and lighted areas and you should do so, because many of the best pictures of Paris can be taken at night of illuminated buildings, or at twilight, when there is still enough daylight to see the outlines of the scene and the lights are turned on. It is safe to shoot at this time because there are a lot of people about and the police are nearby directing traffic or patrolling the sidewalks.

The safest places from which to shoot these night shots.is from the marked intersections, where there are plastic crosswalk protectors that are just the right height to rest your camera on and use as a substitute tripod.

WHERE TO BUY FILM AND HAVE IT DEVELOPED

You can buy film as easily in Paris as in any U.S. city; but it is much better to buy it at home and take it with you overseas. Even though the brand name may look the same, the emulsions are different. For example, the current Agfachrome 64 film is available there, but at ASA 50. Also, if you buy your film in the States with processing included, and try to have it developed in Paris, you will still be charged for development there, and vice versa. Of course, if you buy your film in the States with development *not* included, you can have it developed in Paris.

A good place to take your film processing and to buy accessories is the **FNAC** CAMERA STORES. There are three at convenient locations throughout the city:

- Near the TOUR MONTPARNASSE AT 136 RUE DE RENNES,

- Near the ARC DE TRIOMPHE ETOILE AT 26 AVENUE DE WAGRAM,

- Near the POMPIDOU CENTER AT 6 BOULEVARD DE SÉBASTOPOL.

In addition to carrying a large inventory of photographic equipment, the FNAC stores will send your film out to labs for development and will refer you to local labs and camera-repair facilities.

A local lab that we tested for Ektachrome (ASA 200, 400) and Agfachrome 64 film is: GORNE at 10 RUE VAVIN, which is in the Montparnasse district. (Tel: 633 45 97 or 326 61 16.) There is English-speaking personnel there, as there is in the FNAC stores.

If you are in a hurry for your film processing, specify "professional service," which means 3-hour development.

V.A.T. exemption

Should you buy film or equipment worth over 400 francs, be sure to take advantage of the exemption from the V.A.T. (Value Added Tax), to which tourists are entitled. To qualify for this exemption, ask for a "Bordereau de Vente" form. The store fills this out and gives you the two pink copies. Upon leaving France, you have to give Customs this invoice, which comes in a stamped envelope, and show them the goods that you purchased. Customs then sends back one of the pink invoice copies to the seller, who then will send you a refund of the Value Added Tax that you paid on the purchase. That's the way the refund system works; if you ask why, you will probably receive the same Gallic shrug of the shoulders that we got when we asked.

Some of your best shots may be candids that just happen, such as the back view of this considerate dog-owner giving his tired pet a lift.

CURRENT EVENTS

To find out what's happening in Paris, you can buy a publication at most newsstands called *Une Semaine de Paris Pariscop,* which lists what's going on each week. Also, the Paris Office of Tourism puts out a magazine called *Paris Selection.* This lists current events in English on a bimonthly basis, and you can purchase it while you are picking up your free brochures on other events happening all over France.

THE BEST WAY TO GET AROUND PARIS

First of all, pick up the tourist aids and information at the PARIS OFFICE OF TOURISM at 127 CHAMPS-ELYSÉES. Next, if you

Outdoor art exhibits make good photo material. This display was along the Champs-Elysées.

Paris is famous for its outdoor bookstalls. Expose for the interior, which may be somewhat darker than the street itself. For this shot, a slower shutter speed was used, rather than a wider aperture; the result was some blurred action, but better overall sharpness.

*Move in close to photograph
interesting detail, such as this
sidewalk sculpture. Your picture will be more interesting if
you let the detail fill the frame.*

don't already have one, get the *Michelin Paris* guide (green), as
they have really gone "all out" on their homeground.

If you need a detailed map, look for the special fold-out
sectional "Falk Plan." It has everything, including a list of the
streets keyed to the map and two inserts; one of the surrounding highway system, and another of the métro (subway). The
reason that we like the Falk map is that you can unfold it to show
only the section that you are using, which is a great aid when
driving or riding in a bus or the métro.

You can start out on your own exploring Paris by walking,
using the available public transportation and taxis; but a better
way is to take the all-inclusive 3-hour sightseeing bus tours
offered by the CITYRAMA rapid pullman buses.

We have found that an overall tour of this type is the
best way to get a quick overall view; then later you can return for
a closer look at the sights.

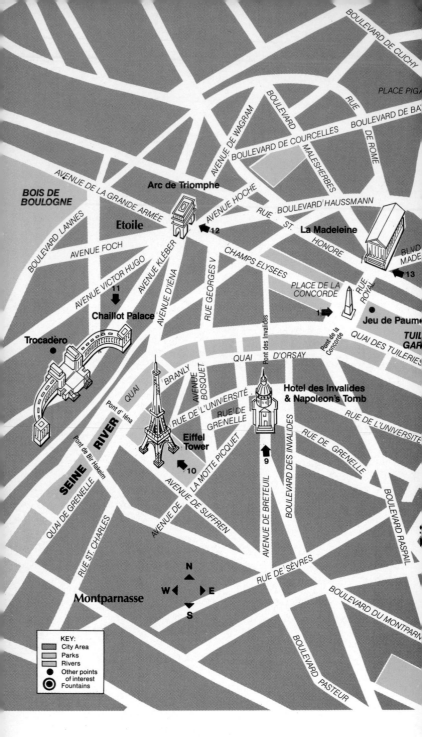

MAJOR SIGHTS ON THE PARIS-BY-BUS TOUR

1. Place de la Concorde.
2. Louvre.
3. Place des Vosges.
4. Bastille.
5. Notre-Dame.
6. Panthéon.
7. Luxembourg Gardens.

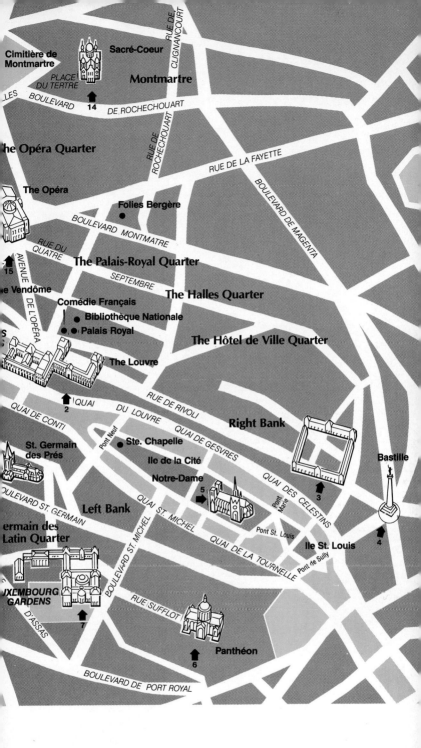

Cimitière de Montmartre

Sacré-Coeur

PLACE DU TERTRE

Montmartre

14

BOULEVARD DE ROCHECHOUART

RUE DE CLIGNANCOURT

he Opéra Quarter

RUE DE ROCHECHOUART

RUE DE LA FAYETTE

BOULEVARD DE MAGENTA

The Opéra

Folies Bergère

BOULEVARD MONTMATRE

RUE DU QUATRE

15

AVENUE DE L'OPÉRA

The Palais-Royal Quarter

SEPTEMBRE

The Halles Quarter

e Vendôme

Comédie Français

Bibliothèque Nationale

Palais Royal

The Hôtel de Ville Quarter

The Louvre

QUAI

RUE DE RIVOLI

QUAI DE CONTI

DU LOUVRE

QUAI DE GESVRES

Right Bank

Pont Neuf

Ste. Chapelle

Ile de la Cité

Notre-Dame

St. Germain des Prés

Bastille

QUAI DES CELESTINS

3

Pont Marie

5

BOULEVARD ST. GERMAIN

Left Bank

QUAI ST. MICHEL

Pont St. Louis

Ile St. Louis

4

ermain des Latin Quarter

BOULEVARD ST. MICHEL

QUAI DE LA TOURNELLE

Pont de Sully

UXEMBOURG GARDENS

RUE SUFFLOT

7

D'ASSAS

Panthéon

6

BOULEVARD DE PORT ROYAL

PARIS BY BUS TOUR

The 3-hour panoramic bus tour offered by the Cityrama double-decker buses is a painless and inexpensive way to get an overview of the picture possibilities of Paris.

◀ *Candid shots of typical Parisian street scenes can be taken during the bus tour if you watch ahead. To be ready for such shots, set your speed shutter, and f-stop and pre-focus your lens, as described in the text.*

▲ *This unusual high-angle view of a sidewalk café was taken on a regular sightseeing bus tour. To take such views, choose the upper level of the double-decker buses and be ready to shoot when the bus is stopped in traffic or waiting for a change of light.*

Departures

The tour starts and ends by the golden statue of JOAN OF ARC in the PLACE DES PYRAMIDES off the RUE DE RIVOLI across from the LOUVRE. There are seven daily departures starting at 9:30 A.M., with the last one departing at 4 P.M. Picture-wise, it doesn't matter which bus you take, because the tour covers the entire city and the lighting may be good on some sights in the morning and on others in the afternoon.

The Sights

Some of the sights you will see (strictly from the bus, no inside visits) are: the TUILERIES GARDENS, the PLACE DE LA CONCORDE, the LOUVRE PALACE AND MUSEUM, ILE DE LA CITÉ, NOTRE DAME, the PLACE DES VOSGES, PLACE DE LA BASTILLE, the LATIN QUARTER, the PANTHÉON, LUXEMBOURG GARDENS, INVALIDES, the EIFFEL TOWER, the ARC DE TRIOMPHE, the CHAMPS-ELYSÉES, MADELEINE CHURCH, MONTMARTRE, the OPÉRA, and the PLACE VENDÔME.

Where to sit

You will be able to take pictures from the bus, especially if you can get a seat on the top deck, preferably in front; from there you have an unobstructed view through the glass. A side seat, however, is also good because you can open the window and shoot when the bus is stopped in traffic or as it makes a turn. In fact, the double decker bus gives you an opportunity for street views of Paris that you can't get any other way. It also gives you added height for picturing the buildings and monuments without tilt in the vertical lines.

Shooting from the Bus

You have to shoot quickly from the bus. There is no time to focus or fiddle with your exposure meter and settings, so you should prepare your gear beforehand.

- Load the camera

- Set your shutter speed to 1/125 sec.

- Adjust your f-stop for the light, and

- Set your focus at the approximate distance that you will be shooting.

This way, when a scene appears, you can shoot quickly before the bus is out of range.

The trickiest part of this procedure is setting your lens for focus. Do this by using the depth-of-field scale engraved on your lens. First, determine the f-stop you will need from the exposure reading at 1/125 sec. with the ASA film that you are using (say the setting is f/8 at 1/125 sec. with ASA 64 film). Then check your depth-of-field scale (if you are in doubt about where it is or how to use it, check the "Tips and Techniques" section); and place the lazy-8 infinity mark within the far-distance setting for f/8 and let the near distance fall as it may. You will find that with a normal 50 mm lens, focus will be sharp from about 20 feet to infinity at f/8. This means that sitting at the double-deck level, you will be well above the street and can shoot at farther distances; so with this technique everything in front of, and to the end of, your scene will be sharp without having to focus. All you have to do is pick up your camera and shoot.

A word of caution: With this technique the image will not look sharp through your lens, but it will be; just trust the depth-of-field scale.

There are several other things to be aware of when shooting from a moving vehicle. Don't brace yourself against the bus window or any part of the interior. If you do, you will transmit the vibration of the bus motor to your camera. So sit loose in a relaxed position and let your body act as a shock-absorbing cushion. Try to take your shots when the bus is stopped or slowed down by traffic. And if you have to shoot while the bus is moving fast, or from the side, and the angle of movement is crossing your lens, speed up the shutter to 1/250 sec. and adjust the f-stop accordingly.

Above all, don't worry if you miss some pictures, or if the light isn't right on others. Remember that you are taking this tour mainly to get an overall look at the sights. If you want really good shots, you can't take them from a bus; and many of the sights have inside views that will be discussed later with suggested shooting techniques.

THE SEINE BOAT TOUR

THE BATEAUX MOUCHES, or riverboats, leave from the EM-BARCADÈRE pier on the RIGHT BANK of the SEINE from the PONT (bridge) DE L'ALMA. (Parking is available by the pier). They offer a river-bank view of Paris with some unique picture possibilities.

Before you snap the general scene, look to see if a passing person, car, or other object can add color and action to your picture. Often just such a chance happening, such as the sightseeing boat passing in front of Notre-Dame will really make the picture.

Departures

These glassy cruisers leave on the half hour from 10 A.M. to 10 P.M. during the summer tourist season, and daily with a somewhat shortened schedule the rest of the year. For reservations, you can call 225 96 10, or take your chances and just get on board. If you have to wait, there are some shots you can take from the bridges of the river traffic and riverside activity.

Where to sit

The best viewing level on the boat is the top deck. From there you can shoot ahead as you approach, or behind, after you have passed the sight. You can choose a front or back seat, or even sit at either side as long as you are sitting on the outside and not in the middle of the row. If the boat isn't too crowded, you can play the odds and move around, choosing the best position for the upcoming picture sight.

The Sights

The route takes you through the very heart of Paris: upstream, around ILE DE LA CITÉ and the ILE ST. LOUIS, with unusual views of NOTRE-DAME; and downstream past the EIFFEL TOWER, of which you can get an excellent and different view. There is a particularly good shot as the boat approaches the PONT D'IÉNA. As you are shooting upward, you can include in the foreground the statuary on the bridge supports to give your picture added interest. On the downstream turn, you can get a fabulous shot of the "STATUE OF LIBERTY" (a small replica of the New York statue),

Bright flags on this bateau-mouche make a colorful foreground for this river shot along the Embarcadère. The Pont de l'Alma is in the background.

As you tour along the Seine you will have the opportunity of photographing modern buildings to show another side to the architecture of Paris.

with the towering modern buildings off the QUAI DE GRENELLE piling up behind it. This view is so reminiscent of New York Harbor and the Statue of Liberty, it is phenomenal. But then, why not? The French were the creators of the original statue.

The Statue of Liberty in New York Harbor was a gift from France. A smaller replica stands in Paris, and can be photographed during your boat tour down the Seine.

The River Itself

Besides the views along the shoreline, there are also opportuni-tunities for shots of other boats and of the many bridges. The bridge arches make effective frames for river views and some-times they line up so that you can shoot through a series of arches across the Seine. Don't overlook details of sculpture and decoration as you pass under the bridges.

Shooting from the Boat

The riverboat cruise doesn't call for any special lenses, as the boat does all the work. You only have to wait until it is in the right position for the view you want. And there's no hassle about being quick on the draw, as on the bus tours. You will have plenty of time to focus and compose.

A skylight filter and a polarizing filter can be useful, since you are over water and the haze and blueness of the atmo-sphere is increased. A skylight is sufficient for the blueness and haze, but if you want startling contrast, use the polarizing filter to deepen the blue sky and cut the water reflections. A particu-larly effective time to use a polarizing filter is when the boat turns around the "Statue of Liberty." Then it is useful for sharpen-ing up the detail in the glass- and metal-surfaced buildings of Grenelle.

Watch how the light shines on the river views. The best light angle is usually from the side so that the fronts of buildings or monuments, or the passing riverboats, will have a three-

Look for detail on the Seine ►
bridges during your boat tour. Use your longest telephoto lens, focus, and shoot quickly so that the movement of the boat doesn't bring you too close and out of focus.

▼

dimensional effect. The next best light is from the full front so that the colors are bright and the sun shines through the haze. The worst light on the river cruise is backlight, because then the image is grayed out and looks grainy.

On long views over the water, you can improve contrast by slight underexposure from your meter readings. On middle-distant views, a half stop under will improve clarity; while on far-distant views that look gray in the viewfinder, a full stop down is better.

Don't use a fast, grainy film, because the hazy effect of the moisture rising over the water will accentuate the grain and your distant views will look fuzzy. A medium or slow film like Agfachrome 64, or Kodachrome 25 and 64, is best.

Again, remember, as with the bus tour, there are some good shots that you can take from the riverboats, but don't assume as you glide by in indolent relaxation, that you have *the* pictures of Paris. You can shoot pictures with a different midstream viewpoint from the boats, and get a good idea of the geographic layout of the heart of Paris.

2. The Wonders of Paris

Paris is full of landmarks and monuments, but there are some so well known that when you speak of Paris you think of these. Therefore, these sights are given special consideration here. Each of these *wonders* is different and presents photographic problems and possibilities. Whether you spend a lot of time, or just take a quick shot, these are the pictures that you will show or remember after you leave; so be sure to include them in your pictorial itinerary.

The Trocadéro overlook is a good place to photograph the Eiffel Tower, especially on a wet day when reflections add an extra touch to the scene.

THE EIFFEL TOWER

This is a landmark of Paris and its best-known monument. Worldwide, it is the highest tower of its kind, and still the best "view from the top" in Paris. In addition to the top views, there are also some good views of the tower itself.

Best View of the Tower

The best view of the Eiffel Tower is from the TROCADÉRO across the Seine at the PONT D'IÉNA. To reach this vantage point, you can either cross the bridge (which is directly in front of the tower), or drive down from the ARC DE TRIOMPHE on the AVENUE KLÉBER to the PLACE DU TROCADÉRO, and from there walk toward the tower between the two wings of the PALAIS DE CHAILLOT to the balcony that overlooks the fountain.

This is your first view as you approach the tower. In the passageway between the buildings, there is a row of gold statues that somehow complements the graceful structure of the tower itself, and makes an effective foreground.

Other Views

From the plaza between the two wings of the PALAIS, you can walk out on a balcony that overlooks the TROCADÉRO FOUNTAIN, and beyond it, facing you across the Siene, rises the EIFFEL TOWER. This is the best overall view. Don't settle for a single shot from here but try for various compositions. If you have a wide-angle lens, include the fountain as well as the top of the tower; and if you have a telephoto, try the characteristic silhouette of the tower alone.

Have some fun with filters: color for unusual effects, or a skylight or polarizing filter to add clarity and drama. You can take other views from the bridge, particularly a clear vertical view of the entire tower, since you will be far enough from it to take it all in.

The best views from the Trocadéro are in the late afternoon and at night when the tower is illuminated. But there are many other views, for the Eiffel Tower stands like a tall beacon over the rooftops of Paris. Two long looks are from the ARC DE TRIOMPHE and the MONTPARNASSE TOWER BUILDING. Other, lower locations are from the PONT ALEXANDRE III and the PLACE DE LA CONCORDE. From there, you can frame the tower with statuary figures and ornate fountains in the foreground.

At the Top

A visit to the top of the tower is a must if you want some of the best views of Paris. Go straight to the top — the third platform. From there you can get close-up views of the SEINE, the TROCADÉRO, and the CHAMP DE MARS; and distant views of SACRÉ-COEUR, the INVALIDES, and even NOTRE-DAME. The day has to be clear for sharp pictures and the time for the best light is in the late afternoon. The reason that we suggest you go directly to the top is because that level closes at 5 P.M.; but after that you can stay at the lower levels until 11 P.M.

The Trocadéro complex makes a very effective pattern shot from the Eiffel tower. It is a nearby view that you can take even on hazy days when the far scenes blank out.

A word on views from heights: Remember that the view flattens as you look out into the distance and the houses and buildings stack up in front of each other. For that reason, your closer views are better. Your camera tilted down at about a 45-degree angle will take in the best perspective. It is said that on a clear day you can see a distance of 42 miles from atop the tower, but that doesn't mean that you will get clear photos at that distance because not only will the perspective flatten out but smog and haze will gray out the view. The only photographic solution is to use a telephoto lens for the distant scenes to bring them closer, a skylight filter or a polarizer to sharpen the

33

One of the views from the top of the Eiffel Tower is the Etoile, the intersection of boulevards around the Arc de Triomphe.

Use your telephoto lens to bring such views closer and to make them more identifiable.

contrast, and an underexposure of one-half to one stop to increase the color saturation and highlight detail.

The best films to use for your long views are the slower, fine-grain color or black-and-white emulsions, because the picture details are small and need all the definition they can get.

The other important aspect on distant views is to compose your picture area around a dominant landmark and make that your center of interest. Don't try to take it all in one shot. Walk around the platform and look for a landmark, and include only the area around it in your picture.

THE ARC DE TRIOMPHE

The ARC DE TRIOMPHE has many picture possibilities, both of the arch itself and from the top, of the surrounding city. The best view is looking right up the CHAMPS-ELYSÉES. The light is right in the morning up to about noon, as this façade of the arch faces southeast; but a sunset picture with the characteristic shape standing in silhouette against a flaming sky can also be very effective. A third choice is a night view with the illuminated structure glowing amidst the colored light patterns of the traffic on the Champs-Elysées.

The red light of sunset reflects on the surface of streets as well as on the tops of cars. Take advantage of this phenomenon by including a backlighted scene as well as the sunset sky, as in this view of the Champs Elysees.

Best Camera Position

The best camera position for any of these views is from the center of the CHAMPS-ELYSÉES, where there are crosswalks marked by chest-high posts with a small island around them. Some of the posts serve as traffic lights, in addition to being a great aid to picture-taking. They will protect you while you are standing on the crosswalk, and make a convenient camera support for long-lens and night-illumination exposures. If you have a tabletop tripod (which is easier to carry around with you than a full-sized one) you can rest the legs on top of the pillars to give you the full height.

There are crosswalks all along the CHAMPS-ELYSÉES. Choose the one from which you can get the best composition with the lens or lenses that you are using. An additional aid to photographing this view is that the center lanes of the avenue

Strong crosslight brings out detail on statuary. The Marseillaise group on the side of the Arc de Triomphe shows how sunlight can be used for this effect.

Added color can be given to night scenes by throwing your lens out of focus on nearby lights of passing cars and street lamps. The Champs-Elysées is a good place to try this technique, which is fully explained in the text.

are closed to traffic because they are used as parking areas during certain hours; therefore, you can get a clear shot without cars obstructing the view.

Night shots

When shooting day pictures of the arch, it is a matter of finding your own viewpoint; but the night shots offer some special possibilities.

The straight shot. You can try a straight shot of the illuminated arch and the stopped traffic lights. To do this, watch the movement of the traffic after you have framed your view and determined your exposure. The average exposure for this night-illuminated scene as well as the others is about 1 sec. at *f*/2 on ASA 64 film, and 1/4 sec. at *f*/2 on high-speed film (ASA 200 to 400). But don't take these exposures as gospel; you may want a different effect, so take some extra shots at more and less exposure to be sure. For this "straight" night shot, wait until the cars are stopped; then shoot.

The streak shot. Another technique is to use a slow exposure and let the headlights and taillights of the cars register as streaks of light. For this effect, stop down your lens to *f*/5.6 and make an exposure of several seconds by holding your shutter open on "B" (bulb). Wait until the traffic is moving before opening your shutter, so that the car lights can draw their own pattern. For these longer exposures, be sure that the camera is held very steady by bracing the tripod with your hand; to avoid shutter movement, use a cable release rather than pushing your finger against the shutter button.

The length of the light streaks will depend on how long you leave the shutter open; and remember that you have to change the f-stop each time you make a change in the exposure time. The way to figure the change in exposure, if your meter is not sensitive enough for this low-light scene, is to remember that each time you double the exposure, you have to close the lens down one stop. That is, if the first exposure is 1 sec. at f/2, then it will be 2 sec. at f/2.8, 4 sec. at f/4, 8 sec. at f/5.6, and so on. If you want extra long streaks of light, then stop down to f/5.6 and hold the shutter open for 8 seconds; this will give you the same amount of exposure as you would get at f/2 and 1 sec.

The zoom technique. A third way of having fun with this night shot is with a zoom technique. If you have a zoom lens you can take an interesting shot by sliding the lens from the longest focal length to the shortest during exposure. To do this, first place your camera on a tripod or some other support. Next, set your f-stop for the exposure on the arch—say at f/4 for a 4 second exposure on ASA 64 film. Now focus at the longest focal length on the arch. Set the shutter on bulb, depress the shutter and make the initial 4 second exposure. Then, while leaving the shutter open, slowly pull back the lens to its shortest focal length and, close the shutter.

If you don't have a zoom lens, you can get a similar effect by turning the focusing ring of your lens from near out-of-focus to far in-focus while you're making the exposure. First focus your lens close, and stop it down to the taking aperture, using the depth-of-field preview button. If you don't know how to do this, look at the lights of the cars through the lens and throw them *out of focus*. You will notice that the pinpoints of light become big balloons of color. Keep your lens focused on the size of the orbs that appeal to you, and make an exposure. Next expose on the same film again, *in* focus. (Check your camera and "Tips and Techniques" for making double exposure.)

To make a simulated zoom exposure, turn the focus to infinity while the lens is open; then close the shutter after you have exposed for the right time. During the exposure, turn your focus smoothly and quickly so that the first, out-of-focus exposure is made and the remainder of the time is used to register the infinity image.

These techniques are not all that easy, but try them. You'll get some unusual pictures that will put spice in your slide shows. They will also give you ideas for other techniques.

The sculptures on the columns of the Arc de Triomphe make excellent close-ups. The best time to take these is in the morning, or at noon, before you go up on top of the arch. Then the light shines across the figures and gives them depth and outline.

At the top.
The view from the top is panoramic. You can shoot down any of the 12 intersecting avenues that form the ÉTOILE. A view down the AVENUE DE LA GRANDE ARMÉE will take in the new buildings of LA DÉFENSE, and a look down the CHAMPS-ELYSÉES will show the PLACE DE LA CONCORDE and the LOUVRE. The visibility will depend on how clear the day is, but your best light is around noon when the sun shines directly into the streets.

NOTRE-DAME

NOTRE-DAME is a visual gem and makes great pictures from the outside, inside, and topside — both in the daytime and at night. The classic day views are:

- a front view, facing the building right on the plaza as you approach the main entrance
- a side view from along the bookstalls on the Seine, and
- a back view showing the buttressed back from the Square of John XXIII.

The light is best on the back in the morning, on the side at about noon, and on the front in the afternoon.

Tie in local color with well-known landmarks. In this photo of the bookstalls along the Seine, the towers of Notre-Dame tell you the location.

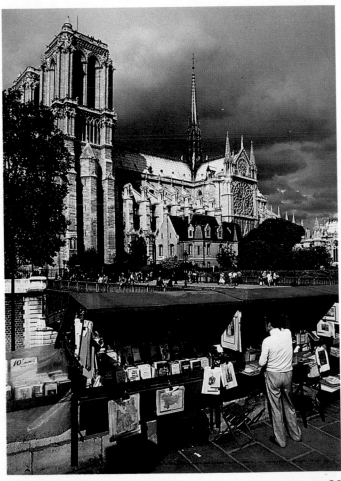

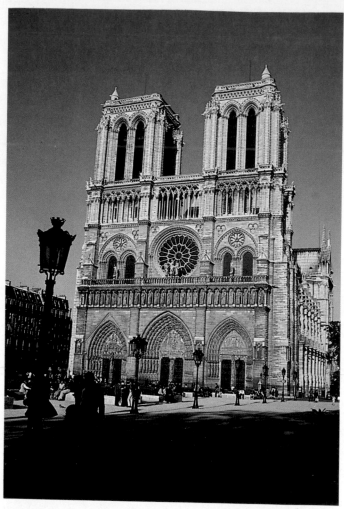

Late afternoon is the best time to photograph the elaborately decorated main entrance to Notre-Dame.

Then the sun shines on the statues and carvings to illuminate the details and give depth to the figures.

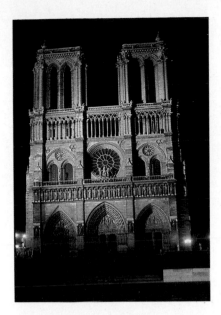

An easy-to-take picture of a night-illuminated scene is the front of Notre-Dame Cathedral. Just brace your camera against the side of one of the lampposts to steady the exposure. Hold the camera vertically so that you can include the tops of the twin towers.

The Outside

The main concern with shooting outside views of NOTRE-DAME is to keep the vertical lines straight. To do this, try standing up on an elevation when facing the buildings. There is a low wall to your right, where the stairs descend to the parking garage. You can use this for added height by climbing on top of it. Another solution is to move back and use a vertical format. Of course, there are exceptions, and you may want a distortion effect; a good one is shooting straight up with a wide-angle lens from the center archway so that the intricate statue-lined arches and the two towers are brought close together.

At night. Notre-Dame is illuminated at night and you can easily take a time exposure even if you don't have a tripod. Just use one of the ornate iron lamp posts in the front plaza for support. Wind your camera strap around the camera and the pole, and tighten the strap around both. This way you will be able to take a 1-sec. time exposure at f/2 on ASA 64 film. Use the self-timer to set off the shutter while holding the camera firmly against the light pole with the strap.

41

Sometimes you should break the rules and point the camera upward. But you should have a reason, such as this overhead view that focuses the attention on the carved statuary all around Notre-Dame's main entrance.

The Inside

Your first picture opportunity indoors is just as you enter by the main door, where there are sound boxes that explain the various parts of the interior. Use the tops of these boxes to brace your camera for an exposure looking up the center nave. Both horizontally and vertically supported pictures are possible. For the vertical views, hold the camera against the side of the speaker boxes.

As you walk around inside, there are more chances for photos. For these, use the columns and sides of archways for support. Be careful how you take a meter reading of the altars with stained-glass window backgrounds. If you are taking in the entire scene at a distance, use a general through-the-lens meter reading; if you are close to the blazing candles of a nearby altar, turn the view so that the candles take up only part of your frame and use that reading to set your exposure for the original scene. (This is to avoid underexposure due to the bright candlelight.)

An obvious picture that you shouldn't miss is a view of the nave as you enter Notre-Dame. Look for a column or use the top of a pew to steady your camera.

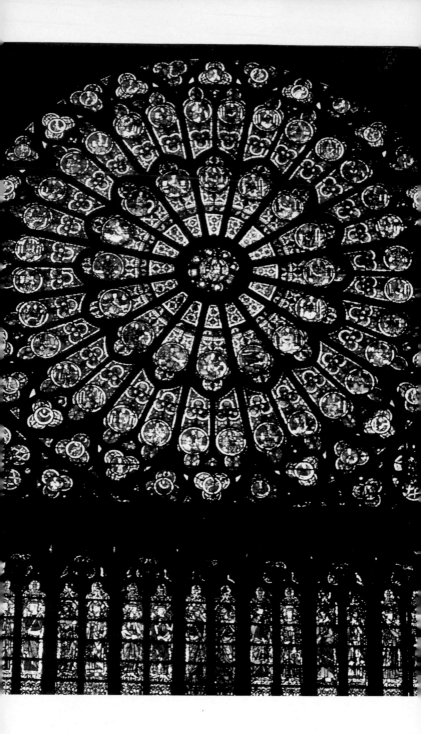

Stained-glass windows. Be sure to line up the stained-glass windows in your viewfinder so that they are square to the camera. This will avoid odd-looking shapes that the architect did not intend. Also, keep the entire surface of the window in focus, because it is all the same distance from your lens. You will notice that the light reading on the stained glass will vary greatly, depending on whether the windows are located on a sunny side or in the shade. To determine the exposure, take your readings directly through the windows from the camera position. The meter readings can vary from 1/60 sec. at *f*/4 with ASA 64 film, on the sunlit side of the windows, to 1/8 sec. at *f*/2.8 with the same film on the shady side.

Candles. You may have some opportunities to snap candid shots of people lighting candles at the altars. For these, be very careful to focus right on the eyes, because you will be shooting nearly wide open and will have very little depth of focus.

The Treasury. There are some good color shots to be had in the TREASURY. The gold pieces are lighted by spotlights inside the cases. By using outdoor color film, you can really make the gold look precious — twice as golden — because tungsten lighting gives a scene a reddish cast on outdoor film. (This

◄ *Slightly underexpose stained-glass windows to capture the richness of the color. This shot of the huge rosette window inside Notre-Dame was underexposed ½-stop .*

There are opportunities for close-ups in the treasury of Notre-Dame. Be sure to move in close so that your picture ❙ *will show the detail.*

phenomenon is also useful for shooting candlelit altar scenes against outdoor lighted stained-glass windows.)

When shooting close-ups of the TREASURY pieces, watch out for glass reflections. Either move to the side to change the angle of reflection, or use a polarizing filter. If the piece is small enough, put the lens right up against the glass.

In the Towers

The Gargoyles. A visit to the Grand Gallery puts you into a Disneyland of gargoyles. You can have a lot of fun shooting the scene below with these outlandish sculptures in the foreground. A wide-angle lens is especially useful for some humorous pictures of giant monsters looking over the city of Paris. For

A bird's-eye view from the top of Notre-Dame makes an unusual picture, especially if you include part of the building to give the scene depth.

The upper balconies of Notre-Dame are decorated with gargoyles that make effective and otherworldly close-ups, evoking visions of Quasimodo and medieval Paris.

this effect, move in close so that the figure fills nearly all the frame except the view below that you want to show. (The view toward SACRÉ-COEUR church is a good angle.) Then use your depth-of-field scale to bring both gargoyle and city scene in sharp focus by stopping down to the smallest *f*-stop (*f*/16 or *f*/22), setting your focusing ring with the infinity mark inside the far focus, and moving no closer than the indicated near focus. You will be bothered some when you look through the lens and nothing seems sharp, but it *will* be. (For more details on this technique, read the "Tips and Techniques" section on focusing).

47

Using the telescopes. There are telescopes mounted on the front balcony roof of NOTRE-DAME. You can use these as super-telephoto attachments and get some fantastic close-ups of far-away scenes like the white dome of SACRÉ-COEUR. To get these views, simply look through the telescope and focus on the scene; then hold your camera up to the eyepiece and focus through your lens at the image. This will work with a normal 50 mm lens. Be sure to underexpose by one stop and bracket your exposures, because distant views tend to fade out.

When climbing to the top of Notre-Dame for an overall view of the city, don't neglect the nearby details, like these statues of saints lining the edge of the roof over the nave.

View from the Towers. It is worth climbing the additional stairs that take you farther up for a view of the back of the church. From there you can get some good shots of the SEINE, including the roof and a lineup of rooftop saints in the foreground.

Notre-Dame is worth much more than a casual snap. Try to budget at least 3 or 4 hours for a complete tour; it's well worth it.

You will need a wide-angle lens to take a close-up of the huge bell inside the tower of Notre-Dame. If your lens won't take in the entire bell, turn the camera vertically and take in as much as you can from the entry way.

THE LOUVRE MUSEUM

The MUSEUM OF THE LOUVRE is enormous; there are over 225 galleries. You can't hope to see, much less photograph, the contents in a single visit, or even in many visits for that matter.

You can photograph in the LOUVRE free of charge and even use a tripod by paying a special fee, but the lighting is poor and you will not get the same results as the postcards you see. Even though you can't do as well as the professional with specialized equipment and special permission, you can still take some very good shots of paintings, statuary, and other art objects; and you don't need a tripod or flash.

Film and Light
Three films are recommended:

- Kodacolor 400 negative film,

- Ektachrome 400 film (daylight), or

- Ektachrome 160 film (tungsten).

You can, of course, use an equivalent film of any other make, but these are the ones that we used.

The reason that both tungsten (indoor) and daylight (outdoor) film are suggested, is that the lighting varies in the galleries. Sometimes it is straight daylight; sometimes it is a spot

Back up far enough from large buildings so that you don't have to tilt the camera upward to include the top, as was done for this shot of the Louvre. Foreground interest was added by including part of the gardens.

Beside the close-ups of art objects in museums, take some overall interior views for contrast. This gallery scene inside the Louvre was made with a slow shutter speed; the camera was pressed against the side of a doorway to steady it.

light; and other times a mixture of indoor and outdoor light. If you don't want to change film for these differing light conditions, the best solution is to settle for Ektachrome 400 film (daylight) and use an 80A filter over the lens when you see that the indoor lighting is stronger than the outdoor light coming in.

We have photographed in the Louvre on the worst possible day when it was dark and raining outside, with very little light coming in through the overhead skylights. In fact, at times the weak lights hidden in the skylight sections were stronger than the daylight. Because of this, our pictures were sometimes blue, and at other times red in tone. So, watch your skylights for best color. On a dark rainy day, the inside lights will prevail; but on bright sunny days, the outside light will be more intense.

The Mona Lisa

One of the photos you will want to take is of the "Mona Lisa"; unfortunately, there couldn't be a worse display for this famous masterpiece, either for photographing or for plain viewing. It is behind thick glass and under an overhang, so very little skylight reaches it. To add to the problem, the glass cover reflects the paintings on the opposite side of the room as well as the viewers standing in front of it.

The solution for photographing the "Mona Lisa" is to return to the Louvre after dark. In summer you can go just before closing at 7 P.M.. At that time the crowds thin out and the daylight is less intense; therefore, the inside lights are stronger. We took our picture from the center of the room and used the seats there

51

If you include spectators looking at a painting, be sure to focus on the painting—not the viewers—so that the eye goes to the center of interest. In this shot of the "Mona Lisa," there is no question as to which part of the picture draws the eye.

to steady the camera for a long exposure of 1/4 sec. at f/2.8 with a 135 mm lens on Ektachrome Film (ASA 160) pushed to ASA 320.

To eliminate most of the reflections, we lined up our viewpoint so that the dark area of a large painting on the opposite wall covered the "Mona Lisa." The picture turned out quite well using this technique; but a longer-focal-length lens, such as a 200 mm, would produce a larger image.

Other paintings

The "Mona Lisa" is a challenge, but the other paintings are much easier to copy. Use the same high-speed film and correction filter, or change the film when the lighting changes. You can handhold your camera at 1/30 sec. and adjust your f-stop (the average exposures will run about f/2.8 at 1/30 sec. on ASA 400 film). Be sure to stand directly in front of the paintings (you can

If you want a square, head-on view of a painting that includes the frame, stand exactly centered in front of it. Line up the edge of the frame with the edges of your viewfinder. This photo of Ingres's "Grande Odalisque" was taken that way.

check the frame against the edges of your viewfinder), hold the camera very steady, and hold your breath as well when making the exposure.

Remember too that you *can* turn your camera sideways when the painting is a vertical shape. Step back and use a longer lens to help straighten vertical lines when a painting is hung above eye level.

You can also shoot a telling detail rather than the whole piece, especially if there is glare over part of the painting that you can't eliminate by changing your camera position.

Occasionally, you may want to take an entire gallery scene. For these, stop down to f/4 for greater depth of field, focus on a painting about one-third the distance into the room, and support your camera against the side of a doorway or a column to steady the longer exposures.

Statues

There are famous statues as well as paintings in the Louvre, such as the WINGED VICTORY OF SAMOTHRACE and the VENUS DE MILO. For the best views of these statues, walk around them and decide which angle you like best. Observe the background as well so that you don't have distracting lines running across the back of your picture. The best way to handle the background and add 3-D to your statue pictures is to pick a view where the light parts of the statue are against a dark background, and the dark areas are against a light background.

Miniatures

There may be small objects or miniature paintings that you will want to photograph. Since such objects are often in glass cases, you can eliminate reflections by putting the lens right up against the glass.

This sidelighted shot of the Venus de Milo is given additional depth and contrast by the dark background. Remember that you can move your camera viewpoint for effects like this.

The Winged Victory of Samothrace is one of the treasures of the Louvre. Walk around it to find the best lighting angle to bring out the detail of the drapery.

Best Time

If you plan to photograph in the Louvre, try to pick a day and time when there are fewer visitors. Otherwise, you will have some long waits at the more popular attractions, such as the "Mona Lisa," before you can get a shot clear of viewers. (On Sunday, admission is free, but it may be worth that 5-franc difference to go another day when there are fewer visitors. It might be worth noting that French schools are closed on Wednesdays, so there might be more children about then. On Tuesday the Louvre is closed. Monday might be a quieter day if there are no big tour buses in. Lastly lunchtime, 12 noon to 2 P.M., are sacred hours to the French—for eating—so you might find the galleries less crowded then.)

This statue of a sleeping nude is beautifully contoured by the light from the window just above it. When exposing for subjects like this, point your meter away from the window to avoid under-exposure.

LE CENTRE GEORGES POMPIDOU

This art center at the Plateau Beaubourg is the latest attraction in Paris, and it is arousing as much controversy as the Eiffel Tower did when it was newly built. The Center is fun to photograph because the exterior is outlandishly colorful, with exposed plumbing and air-duct pipes painted different colors and an outside escalator in red metal and transparent plastic.

The back of the Center—which is really the front because that's where you enter — can be photographed from an open plaza that inclines up to a viewing platform. From there you can shoot over the people's heads. The light is best in the afternoon.

There are many angles and views that you can take of this mixture of plastic, glass, metal, and concrete. It's fun to take the

The outrageous architecture of the Pompidou Center offers numerous photographic possibilities, with its exposed steel girders and huge air ducts.

*When a scene is as obviously
eye-arresting as the Pom-
pidou Center, all you have to
do is back up to include the
entire edifice, choose the
side with the best light, and
shoot.*

escalator to the top and just shoot whatever catches your eye.

A wide-angle lens will help you take in the entire exterior,
as well as close-up shots of the escalator, and various inside
views. There is an open platform on top but it has a limited view
because of the surrounding buildings.

The Pompidou Center is worth photographing, partly because it is a contrast to the rest of Paris.

*Interior shots are easy inside
the Pompidou Center. You
can shoot from the overhead
balconies and brace your
camera on the railing.*

VERSAILLES

Although it is not inside the city of Paris, VERSAILLES is considered a Parisian attraction. It is only a short bus ride out of the city and one can take either a half-day, or a full-day, tour.

Versailles comprises three areas: the PALACE, the GARDENS, and the TRIANONS. You can cover all of these areas on a full-day tour, or if you have more time in Paris, do the Palace and Gardens first and return to the Trianons later.

The Fountains

The FOUNTAINS at Versailles are worth special mention. They are turned on only from 4:30 to 6:30 P.M. on the first and third Sundays of the month. So, if you want to take pictures of them, plan your visit for one of those days.

There are also night illuminations of the fountains and the buildings. For these you have to order tickets in advance by calling 950 36 22, or requesting them at the Paris Tourist Bureau.

Indoors

Versailles has many opportunities for both indoor and outdoor pictures, so take along both regular and high-speed daylight color films when you go.

Don't let the weather stop you from photographing sites to which you may not be able to return. This view of the gardens of Versailles is no prizewinner, but it is a reminder of the day it was visited.

This painting of Louis XIV, in the Apollo Room, was photographed by steadying the camera against the side of a door for a 1/4-sec. exposure at f/2 on ASA 64 film.

You can take pictures on the Palace tour, and there are special rooms that are particularly good for photography. These are listed in the order that you will see them.

The Royal Chapel. The best view is from the balcony overlooking the interior. The light is quite poor; therefore, our exposures were made at 1/15 sec. at f/2 on Agfachrome 64 film. The day that we were there it was cloudy and overcast, so there was very little outdoor light coming in. Use the widest-angle lens that you have for the balcony view and brace your camera against the marble columns for support. The ceiling frescoes make a particularly good shot from the balcony with a wide-angle lens. Simply tilt the camera up and again use the pillars for support.

The Hercules Room. The chief picture subject here is the marble fireplace with a painting by Veronese over the mantle. The ceiling frescoes are also worth including.

You can shoot this interior despite the low light by pressing your camera up against the wall opposite the fireplace for support. First determine the exposure, then focus, cock the shutter, and use the self-timer to set it off as you firmly hold the camera against the wall. Our exposures here 1/4 to 1/2 sec. at f/2 on ASA 64 film. Shoot both a horizontal and a vertical view to show more and less of the ceiling.

The Apollo Room. The circular center painting on the ceiling surrounded by gold figures makes a colorful shot. For this picture, place your camera on the floor, lens up, directly below the painting after setting your exposure, and focus. As in the Hercules Room, set off your shutter with the self-timer while you step back out of camera range. Our exposure for this was 1/4 sec. at f/2 on ASA 64 film.

Note: When focusing from floor level, kneel down and focus at a slight angle for a longer view. That way the straight-up view will be sharp. If you are using a wide-angle lens (which is recommended for all these interior shots), you can simply set the focus on the infinity mark.

The War Room. The best view here is from the side of the doorway leading into the Hall of Mirrors. Use the huge marble column as a brace and take in the view of the stucco relief of King Louis XIV on horseback, the magnificent chandelier, and part of the ceiling fresco.

If you don't have a wide-angle lens, take two shots: one of the plaster medallion and the chandelier, and the other of the ceiling.

The stucco bas-relief of Louis XIV on horseback appears in the War Drawing Room. Choose your lighting angle to bring out the contours.

The Hall of Mirrors at Versailles is a fine place to shoot. For added interest, use the reflections in the mirrors as part of your scene. By placing your camera lens close to the mirror surface, you can take a picture that will appear to be a double exposure.

The Hall of Mirrors. The first good shot is immediately upon entry. Use the columns on either side of the doorway for camera support to take a vertical shot of the ceiling and the long mirror-lined hallway. You will have to watch your focus because this is a very long corridor. For maximum sharpness, stop down to f/4 and use your depth-of-field scale by placing the infinity mark just inside the far distance mark for f/4 and letting the near distance set itself. This technique will give you sharp focus from at least 30 feet to infinity on a normal lens and much closer on a wide-angle. (Look up Focusing in "Tips and Techniques" for more information.)

Use the mirrors lining the hallway for your photography by placing your camera against the mirrored surface so that half of the picture is a reflection and the other half is a long view down the corridor. Or simply shoot the reflections themselves as they appear. You can also take a picture of your own reflection and that of your partner, or group, to show you in Versailles. When focusing the reflection shots, be sure to focus on the reflected image, not on the mirrored surface.

Be careful how you take exposure readings there. There is a great contrast in the lighting between the reflections, the windows, and the recessed ceiling. So take your meter readings from a middle-tone area rather than from bright highlights.

The Queen's Chamber. This is a very dark room and seemingly always crowded by onlookers. You can take a good picture here but a wide-angle lens is necessary because you will be in very close quarters.

Wait until a group moves on and then quickly take your shots by holding the camera against the wall near one of the large window wells. Focus right on the gilded canopy over the bed for best overall sharpness. The exposure, depending on the available light, can be up to 1 sec. at *f*/2 on ASA 64 film, so use the self-timer and hold your camera firmly against the wall.

The Coronation Room. Here is the original of the famous painting by David of NAPOLEON'S CORONATION. This is a very difficult photo to take because of the glare on the painting from the outside windows. The best technique is to use the opposite wall for support, move around until you can eliminate the light reflections, and shoot only the part of the painting that is not "glary."

The Battle Gallery. This collection of paintings and busts of the heroes of France has good picture possibilities. As you enter, you can shoot down the length of the room with one of the busts large in the foreground. You will need a wide-angle lens to get the necessary sharpness.

Busts of the heroes of France line up for a good perspective shot in the War Drawing Room. Focus about one-third of the distance into the picture for sharpest results.

A close-up of a statue in the Battle Gallery gives depth to the general view. To take such a picture you will need a wide-angle lens. See the text for instructions on where to focus.

For good composition, move in close to the bust so that it fills much of the viewfinder and balances the huge paintings on the room wall. Focus by using the depth-of-field scale on your lens so that both the statue and the paintings are sharp.

The lighting in this gallery is quite good and you can copy the large paintings by just choosing a viewpoint and holding your camera very steady. A high-speed color film is best. Ektachrome 400 film (daylight) gives you handholdable exposures of 1/30 sec. at *f*/2.8.

The visitors in this section of the Battle Gallery are dwarfed by the huge paintings overhead. Such contrasts add interest to an otherwise mundane shot.

A tip for middle-of-the-room handheld long exposures is to use the shoulders of a companion, or a member of your group, as support. Ask the person to hold his or her breath while you are shooting, and be sure that you do likewise.

Caution Regarding Exposures: Although we mention exposures for some of the pictures, don't take these as gospel. The day we were at Versailles, it was dark, rainy, and miserable. You may be there on a better day, in which case your exposure times will be much shorter. Even on the same day, we noticed that in some interiors, the exposures differed by two stops or more depending on the angle and direction of the outside light.

Outdoors

The outdoor pictures at Versailles of the GARDENS and the TRIANONS have many views. Look for ways to combine the fountains and statuary with a building background, and be sure to walk around and observe the effects of the light from various positions before shooting. Generally, the light is best for form and color when it strikes the scene from either a front right or a front left angle, so that part is in sun and part in shade. This type of lighting gives depth to the picture. But there are times when backlight is more effective, such as when the sun shines through the water spray of a fountain, or backlights the form of the landscape for a one-dimensional Japanese-print effect.

3. The Ile de la Cité

The most picturesque part of Paris is on and around the two islands in the Seine: the ILE DE LA CITÉ, and the ILE ST. LOUIS. On this stretch along the river banks of the Seine, you will find views of tree-shaded bookstalls, outdoor cafés, lovers, ornate bridges, glimpses of church spires, and building towers.

Although this section of the river is just a little over a mile, don't try to hurry your photo tour. Go slowly and fully explore each area and photo site that we mention.

ILE DE LA CITÉ AND SURROUNDING VICINITY

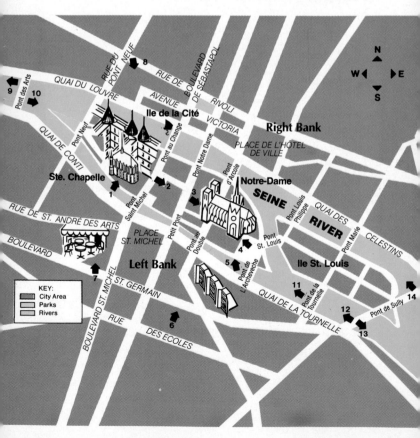

1. Interior views of the Sainte-Chapelle.

2. An outside view as you leave the Sainte-Chapelle.

3. The classic view of the front of Notre-Dame.

4 A view from the back of Notre Dame, showing the flying buttresses.

5. An overall view of Notre-Dame from the Pont de l'Archevêché.

6. A good place to photograph the bookstalls along the Seine, with Notre-Dame in the background.

7. Place Saint-Michel, a good spot to photograph outdoor cafés.

8. The view of the towers of the Conciergerie.

9-10. Views up and down the Seine from the Pont des Arts.

11-14 Other views of the Seine from bridges near the Ile de la Cité and the Ile Saint-Louis.

Sunday is the best day for this tour. Then, it seems that all of Paris comes here to see and be seen, giving you a fine opportunity for candid as well as action shots.

In summer there are festivals, and sometimes the PONT-NEUF is closed and becomes a carnival bridge. Other celebrations are held outdoors in the squares, such as at the PLACE ST.-MICHEL. Check with the Paris Tourist Bureau, or look in the weekly magazines, such as L'Officiel des Spectacles, and Une Semaine de Paris Pariscop for these events.

THE SAINTE-CHAPELLE

This gem of Gothic architecture is a perfect subject for color film. The stained-glass windows are literally side by side giving you a chance to take a wall of color rather than the usual lone window found in other churches.

The Windows
The best way to take views of the windows is to stand on the stone benches that run along the interior walls and use the columns to support your camera. In this way, you will gain additional height that will help to straighten the vertical lines, and by supporting the camera against the columns, you will be able to steady your long exposures.

Shoot toward the windows that are backlit by the sun for the best color, and take your meter readings directly through

To show both the interior and the stained-glass windows of the Sainte-Chapelle, use an exposure setting halfway between the meter reading of the windows and that of the interior.

The unusual color effect in this interior shot of the Sainte-Chapelle occurred because of two different light sources in the same scene. The stained glass windows appear bluish because they were illuminated by daylight, while the gold decorations turned reddish because of the interior's tungsten lighting.

the glass from camera position; use this highlight reading for your exposure. (This subject can be ruined by overexposure, which will cause weak coloring in the stained-glass areas. So use the metered exposure directly from the windows.)

The exposure readings will vary depending on whether the sun is shining or not, and on the depth of color in the glass. Our exposures were at f/2 from 1/8 to 1/2 sec. on Agfachrome 64 film. A faster color film such as Ektachrome 400 film (daylight) would give you a better chance both for definition — by being able to stop down — and for steadiness — by being able to increase your shutter speed. (With ASA 400 film, comparable exposures would be f/2.8 from 1/30 to 1/8 sec.)

A wide-angle lens will enable you to take in larger areas of the stained-glass windows, but you can get some good angles even with a normal lens. Remember to keep your lines vertical by either turning your camera to the upright position, or backing up to a farther distance.

Reflections on the Floor
When the sun shines through the stained-glass windows, there are pools of colored light projected onto the chapel floor. Include these in your composition, or use them to take an unusual color shot of a companion by asking the person to move into the light path. The patches of colored lights on the subject's face will make an unusual portrait.

An additional view
As you leave the Sainte-Chapelle through the outer gateway, there is a fine view of the towers of the COMMERCE BUILDING through the iron grillwork. Move in close to the gate and use the gold crown shield as foreground framing. Focus right on the shield so that it will be sharp in the foreground.

67

VIEWS OF NOTRE-DAME

The full photographic possibilities of **NOTRE-DAME** are listed in Chapter 2, "The Wonders of Paris" but included here are four surefire camera views on the Ile de la Cité. They are indicated on the map by camera positions 3, 4, 5, and 6. Check these views as you walk around the island.

VIEWS AROUND THE ISLAND

The Conciergerie
The **CONCIERGERIE** looks like a turreted medieval castle (which in fact it was) from the **RIGHT BANK** of the Seine. A good view of it is from camera position 8, above the **PONT-NEUF**.

Pont-Neuf
The views from the Pont-Neuf itself offer a variety of scenes, with the towers of **NOTRE-DAME** and **SAINTE-CHAPELLE** thrusting up over the tops of the buildings (camera positions 9 and 10).

Ile St.-Louis
Farther upstream, the bridges over **ILE ST.-LOUIS** make good vantage points for additional views (camera positions 11-14).

The Conciergerie towers look like the walls and turrets of a medieval castle. This view can be taken from a riverboat as it passes the Ile de la Cité or from one of the bridges across the Seine.

Backpackers add a colorful touch to an empty Place St.-André des Arts in the Latin Quarter. Without people in this scene, it would be a rather bleak shot.

The Left Bank

On the LEFT BANK, just off the Pont St.-Michel, you will find one of the most picturesque places of Paris for local color.

Place St.-Michel and Place St.-André des Arts. These squares are the gathering places for students of the LATIN QUARTER. Here and farther up the BOULEVARD ST.-MICHEL are outdoor cafés and second-hand book shops where you can find students and strollers at all hours.

The PLACE ST.-ANDRÉ DES ARTS is an example of a typical Paris scene. The sidewalk cafe is right by the entrance to the métro, which is one of the old ornate gates decorated with fancy ironwork. Two giant kiosks flank the sidewalk tables, and old buildings with chimney pots form the background.

This is an easy picture to take. For added height, stand on top of one of the short concrete pillars that line the sidewalk and use the kiosks to frame the café scene.

Another view is right by the old métro entrance with the restaurant activity in the background. Use the tree foliage to frame the street scene and watch for typical action when the waiters are serving. Sometimes there are street musicians playing; you can include them for atmosphere. The late afternoon is a good time to explore the picture possibilities here, when the light is still good for pictures and the crowds gather for afternoon coffee or an aperitif.

The views suggested on the islands and surrounding areas are not the only ones, but they are good places to start; or if you have very little time, go directly to these spots and shoot.

69

4. Meandering Around Montmartre

The Moulin Rouge cabaret is not only a Paris institution but it has been copied worldwide. This is the original and it is still standing.

If you are visiting Montmartre, it is right on your way; you can just stop and take some pictures. It is on the Boulevard de Clichy at the Place Blanche and Rue Lepic. If you have more time, you can visit this area on a Sunday afternoon for some action shots in the streets, or later in the evening after you tour Montmartre when the lights have been turned on.

The daylight view can be taken right across from the Place Blanche, in the afternoon. The same view is better later in the day when the lights are turned on. For night shots remember the basic exposure of 1 sec. at f/2 on ASA 64 film, or 1/4 and 1/8 sec. on Ektachrome 200 and 400 film (daylight), or Kodacolor 400 film.

If you are near a well-known landmark, take a quick snap of it whether the light is just right or not. At least you'll have a record shot if you can't return for a better one. This photo of the Moulin Rouge nightclub would have been better with the lights on—but only a daytime shot was possible.

THE STREETS OF MONTMARTRE

The narrow, canyon-like streets of this old section make the kind of nostalgic views of Paris that you see in many paintings. This is because **MONTMARTRE** was the bohemian artists' quarter where modern art was born. Many of Utrillo's canvases were painted there. One famous view is the crossroads at the intersection of Rue Norvins, Rue des Saules, and Rue St.-Rustique.

Your approach to picture-taking there should be like that of the original artists. Walk slowly and look for views. Around the **SACRÉ-COEUR** Church and the **PLACE DU TERTRE**, you can see the towers of the church peering over chimney pots and upper story windows with potted geraniums on the sills. Observe the reflection of light on the cobblestone streets. A backlight will accent the texture of the stones and make a contrasting pattern to the whitewashed walls of the houses. Look for outdoor art exhibits right on the street in front of the artists' studios and watch for the artists themselves to include in your pictures.

This area is a good place to try your lenses. Use the wide-angle to move up close to an interesting detail, such as an overhead sign or a storefront, and include the distant street in the background. With your telephoto, search for distant views of windows and chimney pots, or texture of tile roofs with the white towers of Sacré-Coeur in the background. And if you only have one lens, don't let that stop you. It's the view that counts — where you stand and point the camera—not technique.

THE PLACE DU TERTRE

This square, just a block away from Sacré-Coeur, is where you can really capture the spirit of Montmartre in your pictures. There are artists displaying their works and painting and sketching the passersby; old buildings and sidewalk cafés serve as backgrounds to enhance the atmosphere.

Walk around the square and observe the scene; think about what part of it you want to emphasize, and make that your center of interest. If the subject is an artist sketching, then move in close or use your telephoto lens. If it is a view of the paintings in the park and the outdoor cafes across the street, decide which paintings you want to feature and how much of the background scene you want to include; then move to the camera position that will give you that view.

The Place du Tertre is a good place for candids of both French and foreign tourists enjoying the sights. To take these shots unobtrusively, stand in doorways or under awnings where you have a clear view, but will not be easily seen.

This area is best in the late afternoon, or even as the lights are being turned on when there is still sufficient light for pictures. Then you can use a high-speed color film to capture the atmosphere. Use the poles, sides of buildings, or trees to steady your camera. At dusk, you can shoot at shutter speeds of 1/30, or as slow as 1/8 sec. wide open (or one stop down for sharpness) with ASA 200 to 400 film.

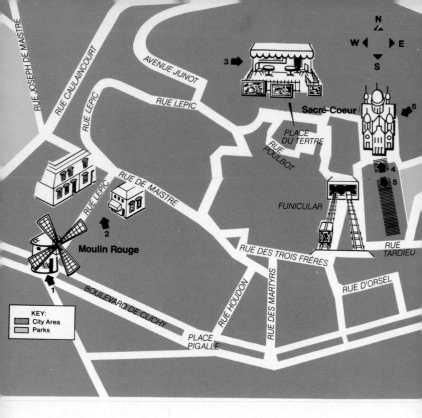

MEANDERING AROUND MONTMARTRE

1. The Moulin Rouge nightclub—a good view by day, even better by night.

2. Scenic views of old cobblestone streets, just as they were painted by Utrillo and others.

3. Place du Tertre, where artists paint and display their canvases while sidewalk café customers look on.

4 and 5. Sacré-Coeur and other vistas of the city, viewed from the overlook at the top of the steps leading to Montmartre.

6. A not-to-be-missed inside view of Sacré-Coeur during the evening mass.

THE SACRÉ-COEUR

The Sacré-Coeur church is the focal point of Montmartre. As you walk through the streets, its white, bulbous towers appear and disappear like a mirage between the rooftops, but the view from the front shows the towers in their impressive reality.

This view is from the overlook plaza terrace by the road that skirts the base of the church grounds. From there you get a symmetric composition looking right up a steep flight of stairs directly at the church.

To contrast the whiteness of the church against the sky, underexpose one-half stop, and for a dramatic effect use a polarizing filter. If there are passing clouds, wait for the sun to

Look for humorous touches, such as this open-topped car with a tourist taking a picture of the Sacré-Coeur.

Large detail in the foreground gives depth to a scene. The outsized chimneypots in this over-all view, taken from the overlook in front of the Sacré-Coeur, give contrast to the miniature scene beyond.

shine through to change the color from a shadowy gray to a sunlit white.

A good camera position for a normal-lens view is from directly across the street.

The city views from the overlook are disappointing; none of the landmark buildings or monuments stands out and the scene has an overall flatness because of the uniformity of the buildings.

There is an alternate overall view of the city from the street that leads around to the left as you are facing the church. This view gives you a chance to add foreground interest by including some nearby houses with giant chimney pots against the background scene.

A further panoramic view can be taken from the gallery of the dome. It is possible to go up inside any day until 6:30 P.M.

The interior of the basilica with its huge painting of Christ, makes a spectacular photo when it is lighted for mass. You can take this shot by supporting your camera against the columns in back of the sitting area, or you can take a seat and use the prayer stand as a support. The exposure for this inside shot is f/2 at 1/2 sec. on ASA 64 daylight color film. On this film the scene will have a reddish-yellow cast (a warm glow). If you want more accurate color, use a tungsten film.

The Sacré-Coeur area of Montmartre is a place for intimate pictures of artistic Paris.

5. Grand Vistas Around the Place de la Concorde

Just as the Ile de la Cité is the oldest section of Paris, and Montmartre is the bohemian center, so is the Place de la Concorde the area for those world famous vistas that are the pride of the city.

From there you can look all the way up the CHAMPS-ELYSÉES to the ARC DE TRIOMPHE, down the TUILERIES gardens to the ARCH OF THE CAROUSEL and the LOUVRE, and across to the EIFFEL TOWER. A short walk will take you to another grand view — the INVALIDES — framed by the elaborate ironwork and statuary of the PONT ALEXANDRE III.

A suggested tour is the PLACE DE LA CONCORDE and the TUILERIES GARDENS, with a long look across PONT ALEXANDRE III at the Invalides, and a rest stop in the JEU DE PAUME museum of impressionist art.

The fountains in the center of the Place de la Concorde offer many composition possibilities. Move in close and fill your camera frame with the fanciful figures; include the Obelisk landmark in the background.

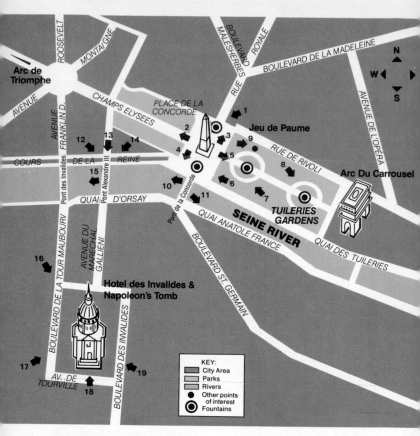

THE GRAND VISTAS AROUND THE PLACE DE LA CONCORDE

1. View of the Place de la Concorde through the side fountain.

2–5. Views in all four directions from the central obelisk of the Place de la Concorde.

6. An overlook of the Place de la Concorde from the terrace of the Tuileries gardens.

7–8. Views both up and down the central walkway of the Tuileries gardens.

9. A picture of the interior at the Jeu de Paume.

10–11. Views up and down the Seine from the Pont de la Concorde.

12–14. A choice of compositions at the head of Pont Alexandre III.

15. A look at the Eiffel Tower through the statuary of Pont Alexandre III.

16.   The garden and cannon side of the Invalides.

17–19.   A choice of views of Napoleon's Tomb and the Invalides.

PLACE DE LA CONCORDE VIEWS

Most long-distance views are a bore. You can stand in the center of a recommended view and shoot straight ahead, and your picture will result in a mediocre foreground with a small center of interest off in the distance. Most of these views need some doctoring; they cannot simply be taken head-on.

The way to add interest is to frame your distant view with a nearby scene, or bring it up close with a telephoto lens. Frame your view with a wide-angle lens so that you will have a sharp interesting detail to "entertain" the eye of the viewer.

View 1
You can take such a foreground view from the north fountain in the Place de la Concorde with a wide-angle lens by moving in close to the pool of the fountain so that the foreground shows the water and the statuary in it, and the background includes the Eiffel Tower and the Obelisk. This view is best in the late afternoon when the sun backlights the water, and it's really magnificent if there is a colorful sunset to paint the scene.

Use the depth-of-field scale focusing technique described in "Tips and Techniques" to make sure that your foreground and background are equally sharp. And don't be afraid to move in close so that the foreground statues are large in the viewfinder. In fact, the way to compose this picture is to fill the frame with the foreground and just leave enough room for your background subjects to show through.

View 2
The view up the Champs-Elysées from the Obelisk is a classic. A medium telephoto lens will bring the Arc de Triomphe closer. You can also support your lens against the railing to steady it if you have a longer telephoto such as a 200 mm. Morning or around noon offer the best light so that the front of the arch is in sunlight.

View 3
An equally good central view is in the other direction down the Tuileries toward the Louvre and the Arch of the Carousel. There are other views from this central location in the direction of the two fountains. Have some fun and try various compositions; use all your lenses for variety.

View 4
A good overall view of the Concorde is from the elevation of the terrace that runs right by the front gate to the Tuileries. You can walk up the ramp on either side inside the gate for this view.

The Eiffel Tower is ever-present on the Paris skyline. It is a good "trademark" to include in your scenes. This view is from the Tuileries Gardens.

THE TUILERIES

Continuing into the Tuileries gardens gives you opportunities to use a park and lake foreground for the distant views. One particularly good angle is in front of the round pool where you will see people maneuvering colorful miniature sailboats with long poles from the shoreline. The kids engrossed in this sport make interesting candids, as does the cartful of model boats waiting to be rented. Use these activities as foreground interest against the background of the ARCH OF THE CAROUSEL.

The lake in the Tuileries Gardens makes an effective foreground for distant views. In this shot, a cartful of miniature sailing boats frames the Arch of the Carrousel.

Move around and look for viewpoints. If there is no wind, you can use the pool reflections to add to the scene. This area is especially good for candid shots on Sunday when the garden is filled with strollers.

If you don't have a particular view in mind, preset your camera so that you'll be ready to snap quickly. Keep your shutter speed at 1/125 sec. to stop action; set your f-stop for the light; and focus the distance on 15 to 30 feet so that you will need only a slight correction before you shoot.

Jeu de Paume Museum

The Jeu de Paume museum is a welcome rest stop in the Tuileries, and it is a relatively small gallery that doesn't take too much time to see. You can take indoor pictures here of the famous impressionist paintings. The light is not good because it comes from side windows rather than from an overhead skylight and creates a glare problem on many paintings. Additionally, some of the upstairs rooms are lighted with a mixture of daylight and spotlights. This is where a conversion filter will come in handy. (Use an 80A filter to convert daylight film to tungsten.)

If you can, change to high-speed daylight film when you go inside the museum; however, you can use your regular outdoor color film just as well. The exposures will vary depending on the brightness of the outside light. Our exposures were from f/2 at 1/4 sec. to f/4 at 1/30 sec. on ASA 64 daylight color film.

The glare problem is especially bothersome on certain paintings; try moving to the side, even though your view will not be head-on, or take in only the part of the painting that is not glary. Sometimes a detail can be just as effective. You can also try your polarizing filter to eliminate some of the reflections.

If you find the paintings difficult to focus on because of the Impressionist technique of using dabs of color rather than distinct lines, focus on the edge of the frame with your focusing ring, or on the signature of the artist.

When shooting inside museums, watch for interesting-looking sightseers to include with the paintings. Photos such as this one taken in the Jeu de Paume Museum, can be made at slow shutter speeds when the onlooker is standing still to examine a painting.

VIEWS FROM THE PONT ALEXANDRE III AND THE PONT DE LA CONCORDE

The nearest viewing bridge from the Place de la Concorde is the bridge of the same name, leading from the Place directly over the Seine. This will give you good views up and down the river; but the bridge to head for is the **ALEXANDRE III** farther downstream. This bridge is a monument in itself and when used as a frame for the **INVALIDES** directly across the river, it combines to make one of the grand vistas of Paris.

Use the statuary at the beginning of the bridge as a frame for the far view of the Invalides. A straight-on camera angle is good, looking right over the bridge, or move to either side and use the marble lions as off-center foreground interests. Your exact position will depend on your lens, but be sure to move in close for a dramatic increase in the size of the lions. The best time for these bridge views is in the cross light of morning or afternoon.

Walking across the bridge will give you added possibilities. Use the ornate iron lamps to frame the **EIFFEL TOWER**, or if the sky has interesting cloud formations, a polarizing filter will give a dramatic stormy sky effect.

The garden view of the **INVALIDES** can be taken from the side of the **PLACE DES INVALIDES**, which is right in front of it. Choose the side view that shows the ancient cannons in a strong cross light. If you have a wide-angle lens, move up close to one and shoot down the line. This view will add the drama of diminishing size.

Use your longest telephoto lens to flatten out perspective and make far-apart objects seem close together. A 105 mm lens does just that to this view of the Alexandre III Bridge, with the Invalides in the background.

A head-on view of buildings and monuments can be made more interesting by including gardens, plantings, or shrubbery in the foreground. In this view, the lines of the Invalides and Napolean's Tomb are given added color by the flowers in the foreground.

INVALIDES—NAPOLEON'S TOMB

The front façade of the Invalides, with the dome of the church rising over the top, makes for impressive views from the square in front. You can take a straight-on shot through the flowers, or one from either side using the statues as a frame. The techniques of using flowers, foliage, or statuary as foreground framing can be used on other monuments as well. A straight-on picture of a building can often be made more interesting and intimate this way. (See "Tips and Techniques" on focusing.)

6. The Opéra District

There is a group of attractions just north of the "Grand Views" area. These start with the MADELEINE CHURCH, which can be seen directly up from the Place de la Concorde. From the Madeleine, it's a straight walk up the BOULEVARD DE LA MADELEINE to the OPÉRA at the PLACE DE L'OPÉRA, then down the RUE DE LA PAIX to the PLACE VENDÔME and the fashionable shops of the RUE ST.-HONORÉ. A stroll down St.-Honoré takes you to the COMÉDIE FRANÇAISE and the PALAIS ROYALE. Each of these sights is a well-known attraction of Paris and all have picture possibilities.

THE MADELEINE

A good shot of the Madeleine Church can be taken from the PLACE DE LA CONCORDE with a telephoto lens; but from there it looks sandwiched in by the surrounding high buildings. A better view is from the square in front.

The Outside
You can stand right out in the center of the square and line up your view. If you want to hold the vertical lines of the columns straight and not slanted, take a vertical view and place the Madeleine on the upper part of your frame. Another remedy is to move back to the next crosswalk so that you are farther away.

The direction of the light is important. The best time is from noon to late afternoon when there is a cross light on the columns and the frieze above.

The Inside
The interior has several picture possibilities. One view of the center nave is just as you enter, which you can take by holding your camera pressed up against the huge bronze door. (See Interior Shooting in "Tips and Techniques.")

A closer view of the main altar can be taken by kneeling in a pew and using the prayer stand to rest your camera on. For variety, use the side altar with the candlelit figure of "Mary" as a foreground. Be sure to stop down for additional depth of field, and focus on the foreground not the back altar; or, if you want both in focus, use a wide-angle lens and calculate your focus with the depth-of-field scale (see "Tips and Techniques").

A basic exposure for these interior views is 1/2 sec. at f/2 on ASA 64 film. If you have faster film, adjust accordingly and be sure to make additional exposures because the light does vary.

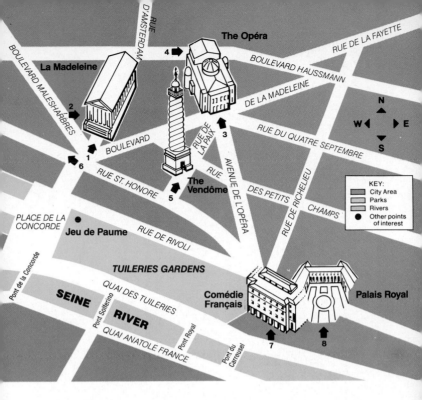

THE OPÉRA DISTRICT

1 and 2.   Views inside and out of the Madeleine Church

3 and 4.   The Opéra possibilities and angles.

5.   View of the column in Place Vendôme, and the best angle for a full shot.

6.   The high-fashion window-shopping tour along Rue Faubourg Saint-Honoré.

7.   What you can take of the Comédie Française without special permission.

8.   A peek into the gardens of the Palais Royale.

Any pattern or design can be used to create foreground interest. The white traffic lane markers add eye-appeal to this simple front view of the Madeleine.

Church altars such as this ► one in the Madeleine are easy to photograph when they are illuminated. Just choose a pew at the right distance and use the top of the seat in front of you, or the prayer stand, to steady your exposure.

Because of their huge size, the bronze doors contrasted with the texture of the marble columns make an interesting detail picture. To show scale, include a person entering or seated outside on the porch.

A candlelighted scene can be photographed by available light. This side altar in the Madeleine was taken with the camera held pressed against the side of a marble column for support.

85

THE OPÉRA

This is the classic "empire-style" structure that dominates the AVENUE DE L'OPÉRA. It is the largest theater of its type and became a model for many others. You have to back away to take in a perspective that shows the top dome rising over the colonnaded façade. Start at the PLACE DE L'OPÉRA; walk away from the building and you can see the dome "grow" to taller proportions.

A straight-on view is sometimes the only one possible, as in this shot of the Opéra, taken from the métro station island in the middle of the street.

The Outside

You can shoot this distant view from the crosswalk two blocks down from the building. Another closer view can be taken from the exit of the métro. If you are athletic, you can climb up on the wall surrounding the exit/entrance; if not, just stand to the side and shoot.

These outside views can be taken around noon or, for more atmosphere, in the evening when the Opéra building is illuminated. For the night shot, use the light poles around the métro station for support on the near view, and the crosswalk traffic light poles for far view. Use the basic night illumination exposure of 1 sec. at f/2 on ASA 64 film, and bracket.

Another outdoor view that captures some of the surrounding atmosphere can be taken from the corner on which the Café

The Chagall fresco on the Opéra ceiling makes a very effective picture. This photo was taken with special permission, which must be obtained from the management.

de l'Opéra is located. You can back off and take in the intersection with both the café and the Opéra; or, if you have a wide-angle lens, move right in close under the awning, stand against the side of the building, and include the café customers in the foreground and the Opéra in the back. For this view, focus on the foreground and just use the characteristic outline of the Opéra in the back.

The Lobby
You can also take some inside views of the lobby of the Opéra. The best time to do this is when attending an evening performance and the lobby is brightly lighted.

Don't make a big thing of interior shooting. Carry your camera unobtrusively in a purse or camera bag with the widest-angle lens that you have. Then, as you walk around before the performance — if you arrive early — or during intermission, simply take your camera out and shoot. Use the many marble columns as support. If you plan to take these indoor shots, load up with high-speed tungsten film — a 20-exposure roll will do — before entering. The main lobby has many good angles that you can take from the balcony above as the theater crowd fills the scene. Open your lens all the way and adjust your shutter in order to stop most of the action and help eliminate camera movement. Focus on the center of the scene; a bright-light area, such as a chandelier, is the easiest to see.

The Auditorium

Photography inside the Opéra requires special permission, but if you wait until the final curtain, you can quickly raise the camera and take a souvenir picture of the Chagall ceiling painting, but not with flash. Use the existing light by setting the shutter at 1/15 sec. and the aperture at $f/2$ on Ektachrome 160 film (tungsten), or you can cut the shutter speed to 1/30 sec. by pushing the film to ASA 320. (If you do push the film, be sure that you take the lobby views at the same pushed setting.)

A way of adding interest to pictures of the Opéra is to shoot from under the awning of a nearby café and include some of the customers at the tables. For added color, wait until a waiter is serving.

*Use the ornate iron street-
lights for dramatic patterns
against the sky. This shot of
the Place Vendôme demon-
strates such a composition.*

PLACE VENDÔME

A walk down the Rue de la Paix from the Opéra to the Place Vendôme will take you past some picture-taking/window-shopping areas. This is where the prestige jewelry shops, such as Cartier, are located.

The displays are well lighted, and you can take shots of the unusual pieces (both in price and beauty) by moving in close and putting your lens as close to the window as possible; most modern lenses can be focused down to 18 inches. If you have to move back, you can stand in front of the reflection area or ask your companion to hold up a jacket, or open up an umbrella (anything dark), to cut down the reflections. This is also a good place to use a polarizing filter, if you have one.

If you are shooting a close-up, be sure to check how sharp the focus is on the object. (To do this, simply depress the depth-of-field preview button and keep stopping down until the entire object is in focus; then adjust your shutter speed to the *f*-stop at which the entire piece is sharp.)

The column in the center of the PLACE VENDÔME can be pictured best with the sunlit side facing you to give relief to the decorations on it and to the statue of Napoleon on top. In addition to the entire view, you can take some close-ups with a telephoto lens of the detailed battle scenes sculptured on the column. Be sure to try vertical views as well as horizontal—the verticals to show the column, and the horizontals to show the square and the surrounding buildings.

The Place Vendôme exits on the RUE ST.-HONORÉ. Take a walk along there for more picturesque window shopping; this time for the high-fashion couturier houses that line the street.

COMÉDIE FRANÇAISE

The outside view of this building is disappointing—not at all like the fanciful front of the Opéra. The best view is from across the plaza of the front façade with the ever-present policeman directing traffic.

Interior pictures of the COMEDIE FRANÇAISE can only be taken with special permission, and shots of the performance are not permitted at any time. This is a shame because the red plush interior makes a dramatic, intimate theater view. (It's well worth seeing a performance; to see the inside even if you don't take any pictures.)

This interior view of the Comédie Française Theater was taken with special permission, but it's typical of the kind of interior views that you can take without special equipment. See the text for details on interior shots.

A very picturesque bookstore with outdoor bookstalls is located directly across the street from the Comédie Française. There you can take some candid shots of typical Parisians looking over the outside offerings. An inconspicuous way to do this is to look at the books yourself while observing the traffic; then take the picture when your subject is engrossed in making a selection.

90

Bookstalls are typical of the Parisian scene. This one is just across the street from the Comédie Française Theater.

Wherever you wander in the city, look for such typical landmarks.

THE PALAIS ROYALE

The central courtyard garden of the Palais Royale is worth a picture. You can try a number of techniques to capture the flower-filled square with the fountain in the middle.

Shoot splashes of impressionistic color by peering through the flowers at the fountain and buildings beyond. For this effect, focus on your distant scene so that the foreground flowers are out of focus. Judge your composition by moving the camera back and forth to get the out-of-focus color spots in the right area of your composition.

An impressionistic effect, such as this one of the Palais-Royal, can be obtained by moving in close to

the clusters of flowers and focusing through them on the scene beyond.

For a long shot of the Palais Royal gardens that has everything in focus, stop down your lens as far as possible, set your shutter speed accordingly, set your focus with the depth-of-field scale markings on your lens, and move back a little farther than the near-distant focus for your position.

Another everything-in-focus technique is to stop your lens down as far as it will go — f/16 or f/22 — and adjust the shutter speed to the lens opening. Set your focus with the depth-of-field scale markings on your lens (see "Tips and Techniques"), and move back just a little farther than the near-distance focus for your camera position.

The people sunning themselves around the garden can also be subjects. To be unobtrusive, use a telephoto for these candids.

7. Other Picturable Sights

Paris has many other sights besides the ones listed here. Some are new and some are old. Among the new is the MONTPARNASSE TOWER, and examples of the old are the LUXEMBOURG GARDENS and the PLACE DES VOSGES. Picturing these sights calls for a range of photo techniques that you can apply to other similar points of interest in the city.

MONTPARNASSE TOWER

From the top of this building among the bohemian cafés you can take some new views of Paris. The rooftop observation platform above the 56th floor is reached by express elevators. The fee at the time of this writing was 8 francs (5 francs for children under 10). The price is well worth it on a clear day; but if it is smoggy or foggy, forget it because all of the views are distant and gray.

There is a handy directional guide on the wall of the open top observation deck. Use this as an aid in identifying the view. The views from the Montparnasse Tower are not as good as the ones from the Eiffel Tower or the Arc de Triomphe, because the landmark sights are all at a distance; this makes it difficult to find a center of interest. The two exceptions are the views toward the EIFFEL TOWER and the SACRÉ-COEUR cathedral.

As in all big cities today, the atmosphere of Paris is hazy. To cut the haze, use a 1A skylight filter for color, or a polarizing filter to add contrast.

A Tip: The windows of the enclosed viewing room on the 56th floor have tinted glass that acts as a filter for the outdoor scene. If you don't have a filter with you, take a look through these downstairs windows after photographing the view from the open rooftop. The haze-cutting effect of the tinted glass will act as a filter for your pictures as well; so shoot a few scenes through the tinted glass if it is not clear outside.

While you are in the area of the Montparnasse Tower, look around the streets, especially on Boulevard Montparnasse just in front of the Tower building. There are sidewalk cafés that are very picturesque and easy to photograph. When shooting, stay back in the shade of the trees that line the boulevard and use the foliage for framing the view.

LUXEMBOURG GARDENS

This elegant garden of flowers, pools, and statuary is near the TOWER MONTPARNASSE. There you can get some chateau-like vistas right in the heart of Paris.

The PALAIS DU LUXEMBOURG that dominates the gardens is the seat of the Senate of France. It may be visited, but the gardens offer more picturesque scenes.

The Medici Fountain

The Medici Fountain on your right as you face the Palace can be taken from the end of the long pool that is surrounded by trees. The trees and the dark water provide a frame for the group of statues at the end of the pool.

The Pool

The large pool in front of the Palace can be used as a center of interest for views looking up toward the observatory, as well as a foreground for shots of the Palace. An effective technique is to shoot very close to the water if the pool surface is calm, and take a mirror image of the building beyond.

The Paths

A walk along the paths reveals many statues that stand out in white relief in the encircling greenery. Watch also for candids of strollers and lovers.

The opposite end of the central esplanade looking toward the observatory also offers vistas of flowers, trees, and statues. Try a telephoto lens for a compressing shot, or a wide-angle lens for a view through the ornate iron gate.

◄ People can add human interest to an otherwise dull picture. This relaxed youth in the Luxembourg Gardens accents the peaceful park scene.

►

A street parade was another unexpected view. By having a camera handy, you can quickly snap scenes such as this before they disappear.

PLACE DES VOSGES

This is the oldest existing square in Paris. VICTOR HUGO'S former house—now a museum—is there. The bus tour passes it, barely squeezing through the narrow street alongside the gardens. You won't be able to take a good picture from the bus, but the return trip is photographically worthwhile.

Try for compositions of the ornate lamp posts against the surrounding seventeenth-century buildings. Close-ups of the architectural features, such as the steep slate roofs pierced with dormer windows and the elaborate chimney pots, also make interesting detail shots. The statue of Louis XIII in the center of the square can also be used as foreground interest for the background house façades.

The Place des Vosges is worth a visit, as it is an example of the architecture of the early 1600s.

HOW TO TAKE PICTURES OF THE UNEXPECTED

It's a curious fact that the unexpected often makes a better picture than the subject you purposefully set out to shoot. The chance scene on the street, an accident of light, or an event you didn't know about can suddenly confront you with a picture possibility. So be ready at all times with your camera loaded, the shutter set at 1/125 sec., and the f-stop adjusted for the light. This doesn't mean that you have to lug all your gear in a heavy gadget bag like a pro; but whenever you go out, take your prepared camera with you for that surprise shot.

Unexpected sights, such as this wedding party in a Rolls Royce preparing to leave the church, make easily taken candids. We just joined the group of bystanders who were watching the scene, and snapped.

Parisian Weddings

An example of the unexpected on Parisian streets is one of the many weddings on Saturdays. On this day, look at the churches you pass for signs of a wedding party. We found one right on the PLACE VICTOR HUGO, where the couple came out of the church and entered an ancient but gleaming Rolls Royce laden with flowers and driven by a top-hatted chauffeur. At the time we were not touring for pictures, having just left the house of a friend; but we had our cameras with us, and took some good pictures of a typical Parisian custom: the "Saturday wedding."

A Procession

On another occasion, while in an apartment visiting again, sounds of a parade startled us. We looked out the window and saw a procession of children on ponies. Luckily, our cameras were nearby and the view could not have been better.

Boats and Fireworks

The highlight of our "chance" pictures of Paris was a parade of lighted boats that drifted down the Seine during one of the summer festivals. The lighted boats didn't make very good shots because of the movement; but the finale did: a fleet of boats spewing fireworks that reflected in the water and lit up the sky. We were again able to take the picture simply because we were there with our cameras ready.

If you should have a chance to shoot a fireworks display, keep a very simple technique in mind.

- Open your lens to *f*/2.

- Set the shutter on "B."

- Support your camera against a wall or on a railing where you can make an exposure without moving.

- Open the lens for a series of fireworks bursts.

- Close the lens.

- Advance the film.

- Repeat for another round.

The *f*/2 recommendation is for average daylight color film from ASA 25 to 64. If your camera is loaded with fast film (ASA 200 or 400), then stop down to *f*/4 and use the same system.

A railing or a wall is recommended for support for the unexpected shot. For planned fireworks photography you are far better off with a sturdy tripod.

This fireworks display during a summer festival on the Seine was taken without using a tripod. The camera was supported on top of a bridge railing; the lens was set open on "bulb" at its largest aperture, and closed again after a pattern of fireworks exploded.

Tips and Techniques

The tips and techniques listed in this section are based on extensive on-assignment travel photography experience. They deal with particular picture problems referred to in the text. This section will also serve as a field guide to special photographic questions that might arise during your travels.

ASA—WHAT IT IS AND HOW TO USE IT

The ASA number on your film package tells you how sensitive the emulsion is to light. The lower the number, such as ASA 25, the less sensitive the film is to light; the higher the number, such as ASA 400, the more sensitive it is.

Photographers refer to this light-sensitivity as the "speed" of the film and refer to the film as "slow" (a low-numbered ASA) or "fast" (a high-numbered ASA). In all cases, the slower the film the finer-grained it is and the better the color rendition and resolution. The faster films are always grainier, even if the color looks just as good.

For general shooting, choose a medium-speed film. In color, use ASA 64, and in black-and-white use ASA 100 for best all-around results.

If you are very particular or you want to have big enlargements made from your negatives or transparencies, then use the slow emulsions like Kodachrome 25 for color, and Panatomic-X for black-and-white.

There are times when you need a fast film because you want to photograph in low light levels, or to stop action. Then you should change to a film with an ASA of 200 or higher.

Each time you double the ASA of the film, you can close your lens down one stop, or use the next higher shutter speed. For example, if your exposure on ASA 64 film is f/4 at 1/30 sec., by changing to ASA 125 film, you can either stop down nearly to f/5.6, or increase the shutter speed to 1/60 sec. and open up slightly from f/4.

ASA–DIN CONVERSION CHART

ASA AND DIN FILM SPEEDS

ASA	DIN	ASA	DIN	ASA	DIN	ASA	DIN
6	9	25	15	100	21	400	27
8	10	32	16	125	22	500	28
10	11	40	17	160	23	640	29
12	12	50	18	200	24	800	30
16	13	64	19	250	25	1000	31
20	14	80	20	320	26	1250	32

BRACKETING

Bracketing is insurance to make certain that you get a good exposure. The pros use this technique, and you should too when you're in doubt about your exposure.

The procedure is first, to make an exposure as your meter indicates. Then, make additional exposures over and under your meter reading. How many additional exposures you need for insurance depends on the subject; but usually two over and two under will give you a good bracket.

You can change either the shutter speeds or the f-stops when you bracket. The choice depends on whether you want to keep the f-stop for sharpness, or the shutter speed to stop motion. For example, if your basic exposure is f/8 at 1/30 sec., to keep your depth of field, increase your exposures by changing shutter speeds down to 1/15 sec. or 1/8 sec., or up to 1/60 sec. or 1/125 sec. instead of changing your f-stop. If, on the other hand, you want to maintain the shutter speed to stop movement, then change your f-stop down to f/5.6 or f/4, or up to f/11 or f/16.

Use the bracketing technique when you don't have a meter, when the light is too low to get a reading, or when the subject is too far away to meter.

Bracketing or taking more than one exposure is a good way to insure that you get your picture. This scene in the Place des Vosges in Paris was shot a number of times to capture the movement of the pigeons — then the best picture was chosen from the take.

CANDIDS AND CHANCE ENCOUNTERS

There are some pictures that you do not anticipate or cannot set up; they are the ones that just happen and you have to be prepared to take them when they do.

Chance Encounters
The technique for photographing the unexpected is to be prepared beforehand.

To be prepared for chance encounters, preset your shutter speed at 1/125 sec., take a light reading, and adjust your f-stop accordingly. Set your lens focus to the distance at which you most frequently take pictures—say 15 feet. This way, as you are touring and walking around between sights, when you see a passing scene, you can just raise your camera to your eye and shoot.

Candids
Candids of people in action, like a peddler selling umbrellas from a pushcart on a rainy day, also call for camera preparation. In this case, focus on your subject, set your shutter speed and f-stop, wait for the right moment, and shoot.

It takes practice to shoot candids and to take advantage of chance encounters. Don't be discouraged if you miss some; keep trying.

CHANGING FILM IN MIDROLL

Sometimes, after you have begun to shoot a roll of film, a new picture opportunity occurs that calls for a different kind of film. These new pictures do not have to be missed because you don't want to lose the unexposed part of the film in your camera. You can change your film and reshoot the roll later.

The way to do this is to note the number of the last exposed frame and rewind the film, stopping just short of pulling the leader back into the cassette. You will know when the film is off the take-up spool, because there will be a sudden loosening up of the tension. At that time, take the film out and write the number of the last exposure on the leader.

When you want to finish the started roll, insert it into the camera as you normally do, cover up the lens with the lens cap, or your hand, and click off the exposed number of shots, plus one. (The extra one is your insurance that you are past the exposed section.) Then you can go ahead and finish shooting the remainder of the roll.

COLOR SATURATION

The ideal color transparency is just on the edge of underexposure so that it has as much detail in the highlight areas as possible. This kind of transparency is said to have full color saturation.

The easiest way to achieve this kind of exposure is to increase your ASA rating by one-half stop. This means that with ASA 25 film, you would set your ASA dial for 32 instead of 25. This can be done because there is a built-in safety factor in the ASA rating of films; you can be a little underexposed, or a little overexposed, and still get a good exposure.

If you reset your ASA for full color saturation, you have to be extra careful with your metering because you no longer have the safety factor. Unless you are very practiced, this system is not appropriate for general shooting. But you can still use it on occasion, by making an extra exposure one-half stop down from your meter reading if you think the picture would be improved by full color saturation.

Underexposed Distant Scenes

When taking distant views, a good rule of thumb is to under-expose from one-half to one full stop from your meter reading. This will give better and deeper color saturation in the highlights —the light parts of the scene.

CUSTOMS (UNITED STATES)

If you are leaving from the States, register your camera equipment—that means bodies, lenses, and all accessories— with the U.S. Customs Office at your local airport or point of departure. You have to take your gear there and have it person-ally verified as to description and serial number; and fill out Form 4457 (long) or Form 4455 (short) on all items you are taking out of the country. The purpose of this registration is so that you can prove on your return that you did not buy the equipment overseas.

Call your local Customs Office to find out when and where this can be done. In most large airports the registration offices are open from 8 A.M. to midnight, so you can go at your conven-ience before departure instead of waiting for the last-minute rush.

When you register your equipment, be sure to pick up the latest list of import duties and restrictions on trademarked equipment that you can legally bring back. This list will be useful if you plan to purchase photographic equipment over-seas, because it shows the amount of import duty you will have to pay. These duties vary; lenses are currently assessed at 15 percent and camera bodies at 7.5 percent.

The trademark import restrictions apply to some brands of cameras imported to the United States. You can only bring back a limited number of these cameras and lenses, even if you did pay for them overseas and are willing to pay the import duties on your return.

DEVELOPING FILMS

When you have taken an unusually large number of photographs far away from home, you will want to take great care when the time comes to develop them. Here are some practical precautions. If you send your films out to be processed:

- do not send them all at once, but in 4 or 5 batches
- divide the batches to include different places and times
- have the first batch developed and view the results before you have any more done. (Although it is rare, machines do break down in commercial labs, so it is safer not to have all your films in at one time. This method also gives you the chance to ask the lab to compensate in future rolls if you notice that you were consistently over- or underexposing.)
- have the rest of the batches processed at separate times.

If you develop the films yourself:

- again, divide the rolls into batches
- do not try any new processes — use the method you know and are comfortable with
- use fresh chemicals
- run a test roll—maybe even two
- when you are satisfied with the test results run the rest of the films through, a few at a time.

These precautions will make you wait a little longer to see your results, but the insurance they offer is more than worthwhile.

DOUBLE EXPOSURES

Double exposures can be achieved in two ways: You can take them in the camera or you can sandwich slides together and copy them onto another slide.

To make double exposures in the camera, you have to be able either to stop the film from advancing so that you can make another exposure on the same frame, or to rewind the film accurately so that the next exposure fits over the previous exposure. With some 35 mm cameras you can simply depress the rewind-lock button (usually on the bottom of the camera) while making a succession of exposures, because then the advance lever will cock the shutter but not pull the film through. With other models you must first shoot, then rewind the film normally one full revolution, and then shoot again.

When you are double exposing in the camera you will need to underexpose one stop for each exposure you make, unless one of your photographs has a dark area into which you plan to place a lighter subject for the next exposure. In this case you can expose normally for both.

If you intend to sandwich slides together later, you should plan for it by overexposing the photographs when you take them so that the final result will not be too dark.

Sandwiching slides together does have the advantage that you can do it on a light table and see what effect you are getting. When you double expose in the camera you cannot always be sure that your subjects are lined up correctly.

A good view of the Eiffel Tower can be taken on the river-boat tour of the Seine. This is a wide angle shot just as the boat goes under the bridge leading to the Trocadéro Gardens.

EQUIPMENT—CHOOSING WHAT YOU WANT

Choosing cameras, lenses, and accessories is a highly personal affair. What works for one photographer may not suit another. The way to choose your photographic equipment is first to decide the *kind* of pictures you want to take, and how much of your energy is going to be put into photography.

You should also consider what *kind* of photographer you are. If you're the type who only wants to take the occasional picture—with a minimum of fuss—to show where you've been, then the simplest camera will do; preferably the one you now have, because you are already familiar with it. If you are an avid snapshooter and have a greater interest in picture-taking and want to shoot enough for a good album display or a slide show, then you will need more equipment. Finally, if you are really serious about photography, and are an advanced amateur, semi-professional, or professional, you will want enough equipment for outstanding pictures, and different equipment for each type of picture-taking situation.

110 Cameras

For the first category, the simplest and easiest cameras to use are the popular, pocket-sized **110 CAMERAS**. They are now produced by a number of different manufacturers at prices ranging from $20 to over $200.

The desirable features on these are the zoom-telephoto lens and the built-in electronic flash.

New 110 cameras are now also on the market with interchangeable lenses and all the features of the 35 mm single-lens reflex (SLR) cameras. You should look at these if size and weight are a travel consideration.

The miniature 110 is suitable for snapshot-size enlargements, photo-album displays, and projection with the new 110 projectors.

Rangefinder Cameras

For the step up into more serious *35 mm* photography, you have a choice between the rangefinder and the SLR types.

Of these, the simpler and less expensive are the **RANGE-FINDER CAMERAS** that come with a fixed lens in the 40 mm range, which gives a slight wide-angle result. These are fine for all-around shooting, but you will tire of them after a while because you can't change the lens and there isn't much room for creativity.

The price range on these simple 35 mm cameras is comparable to the 110's, and they are a better investment if you want image quality rather than portability.

The SLR Camera System

The obvious choice over the fixed-lens rangefinder 35 mm camera is the single-lens reflex (SLR). Through-the-lens viewing shows the picture exactly as you're going to take it, and technology has brought these cameras down to a size and weight that is comparable to that of the rangefinders. Because the SLR is such a popular camera, you have a wide range of choice in features, lenses, and price. But a little common sense will help you make a decision.

Ask yourself, "What am I going to do with the pictures?" "How far into photography am I, and how far do I plan to go?" If the pictures are for yourself and not for the competitive photo market and if you plan to make only normal (that is, up to 16" × 20" enlargements), then you could settle for any of the less-expensive competitive brands. If you can define your aims in photography and know that you'll be satisfied with good results from a limited number of lenses, then you don't have to go for the line that has the most options.

A good way to start an SLR system is to buy the body only (without the 50 mm normal lens that comes with it) and a wide-angle and a telephoto lens. The 50 mm is the one that you will use the least; you will always want to go wider or longer, so why not start out that way?

A good all-purpose wide-angle that will even double for the 50 mm is a 35 mm lens. A moderate telephoto that is just right for portraits and general shooting is the 85 mm lens. We recommend these two as a start.

Of course, you have other options. If you keep the 50 mm, then you should buy a wide-angle lens of 28 mm or an even wider-angle 24 mm. You could also increase the range of the telephoto up to 105 mm or 135 mm. Or, you can opt for a zoom lens and have a combination of focal lengths in one lens. This is an advantage, and a zoom lens is fun because you can frame your image as desired at any focal length without moving toward or away from your subject.

For the serious picture-taker, the sky is the limit, and we won't even talk about price. Here is where the lens options really start. The trick, however, is to buy slowly, before you are over your head. After you have the gear recommended for the intermediates, choose each succeeding item carefully and think of the use you will make of it before you buy.

When expanding your lens system, keep in mind two lenses that are real workhorses: the 20 mm wide-angle and the 200 mm telephoto. The 20 mm wide-angle lens is great for interiors because it's the last stop before you get to the line-bending fisheyes, and the 200 mm telephoto lens is the most practical handholdable focal-length lens for those long shots.

Besides the extra lenses, you should consider an extra camera body. This has many advantages. It will enable you:

- to keep two kinds of film loaded

- to have two bodies ready for fast shooting with a lens on each

- to have an extra camera if something should go wrong.

Accessories

Besides the camera equipment, you should have the following accessories:

- A good *tabletop tripod*. (Get one that is really sturdy; it's worth the extra money.)

- Basic *filters* needed for color photography: a **1A SKYLIGHT** filter to warm up scenes with excessive blue, such as aerials, snow scenes, and overcast cloudy daylight; a **POLARIZING** filter to eliminate reflections, cut down glare, and darken a blue sky without changing the color of the scene; an **80A** filter to convert daylight film to tungsten; an **85B** filter to change tungsten film to daylight; and a **TIFFEN FLD** filter to correct fluorescent light on daylight film and an **FLB** filter to do the same on indoor tungsten emulsion. We also recommend that you keep a **UV** (ultraviolet light absorption) filter on each lens to protect it from dirt and scratches. This filter won't affect the color or exposure. (See itemized filter list in this section.)

- A small *jeweler's screwdriver* is useful for those occasionally loose screws. (The blade of a Swiss Army knife can be honed down to a small screwdriver size.)

- A small plastic bottle of *lens-cleaning fluid* and a packet of *lens-cleaning tissues* are essential. In addition, carry a *lens brush* to flick off the dust. It is not a good idea to rub the lens too much; you might damage the lens coating.

- A small, simple strobe *flash unit* that you can carry in your gadget bag should answer your flash needs. This will do for the occasional flash shot, and this book will tell you how to take pictures in practically all situations without flash where you may have thought that flash was indispensable (see "Flash—When and How to Use It" in this section).

- At this stage, you have to consider a *gadget bag*. It should hold all of your equipment, all of your accessories, plus have some room left over for film, maps, a notebook, and this book. It's a good idea to take all your gear with you when you go bag shopping to see if it all fits before you buy.

There is a bottom line on equipment that may help you keep it in perspective: remember that equipment alone is not going to get you the picture. Only *you* can choose what you see and direct your camera to take it.

EQUIPMENT CHECKLIST FOR TRAVEL PHOTOGRAPHY

You should take the following equipment with you to cover all the picture possibilities explained in this book.

Camera

- We recommend an SLR camera that will accept interchangeable lenses.

Lenses

- A 35 mm lens for general shooting (or a 50 mm lens)
- A 24 mm wide-angle lens (or a 28 mm lens)
- An 85 mm medium-telephoto lens (or one up to 105 mm). (In addition, you can substitute a zoom lens that covers these focal lengths or adds to them.)

Filters

- 1A skylight filter
- Polarizing filter
- 80A and 85B conversion filters
- Tiffen FLD and FLB fluorescent-light correction filters
- UV (ultraviolet absorption) filters
- Additionally, for black-and-white photography, a K-2 yellow, an orange, and a red filter.

Tripods

- You'll get by with a tabletop tripod, but get a sturdy one.

Accessories

- Lens-cleaning brush
- Lens-cleaning fluid
- Jeweler's screwdriver or substitute
- Cable release for long exposures.

Gadget Bag

- Get this last and see if all your gear fits. Don't buy one that looks so ostentatious that it screams, "there is valuable equipment inside!"

Film

- The bulk of your film needs should be covered by a medium-speed color film, like Kodachrome 64, or its equivalent in other brands.

- Extra film should be Ektachrome 200 and 400 film (daylight) for outdoor dim light and indoor daylight shooting, and Ektachrome 160 film (tungsten) for indoor photography.

- Added to this, you can take some rolls of Tri-X black-and-white film. Substitutions can be negative color films, such as Kodacolor II (ASA 100), or Kodacolor 400 film.

- To estimate film needs, multiply your anticipated normal day use from past experience by the number of shooting days on the trip.

EXPOSURE

Exposure is one of the greatest problems in photography. No matter how accurate your meter is, or how automated the camera, there are always exceptions in determining the right exposure.

Exposure meters are calibrated to give you the best reading for the middle tones of the average scene. This means that the exposure reading for the frontlighted picture will be accurate, and you will get maximum tonal values of light and dark according to the capability of the film. But if you are up against an "unaverage" lighting situation, the meter gets confused and you have to help it out.

Backlighted or sidelighted scenes, or landscapes with large areas of dark and light, such as sky or snow, will throw your light meter off. You will get a correct reading for the lightest areas, but the rest of your picture will be underexposed. In these situations you can still enlist the aid of your meter to give you correct exposure, but you have to direct it to give you the information you want.

If a person is backlighted and you want detail in the face, move in close with your meter to cut out the backlight, and take your reading off the face. If you want a silhouette against the setting sun, then point the meter at the sunset and let the figure go black.

The same is true of beach scenes with large areas of light reflecting sand, and of snow scenes with blinding white landscapes. Again, you have to decide what you want to say with your picture and meter accordingly.

In a beach scene, if you want the texture of the golden grains of sand, take a reading of the sand; if you want the figure under the beach umbrella, then direct your meter under the umbrella. The same holds true for snow scenes: To capture the sheen of light reflected off the white snow surface, you must meter exactly that; to show the features of your friend skiing, move in close and determine the exposure for the figure. In each case you have to decide which part of the picture is the most important and make your exposure there.

Warning: Be especially careful in determining exposure for scenes where a light source is shining directly into the lens. Sunsets and spotlighted show scenes are especially difficult. The solution is to move the lens view so that the light source does not shine into the lens but just off to the side. Take the meter reading from this just-out-of-the-light view then swing back for your original composition.

Views from the Eiffel Tower are many and varied but unfortunately often the air is not clear. To cut haze and correct the color use an A-1 Skylight filter and underexpose 1/2-stop. For more clarity use a polarizing filter.

FILM

Choice of film is just as highly personal as the choice of cameras and lenses. But there are some guidelines. You should choose your film, as you choose your camera and lenses, with the end product in mind: your pictures and what you want from them.

If you are shooting a subject that calls for sharpness, or critical color balance, then you should use the slower, fine-grain films. But if you are going after mood or action in poor light, then you need fast films, or those that can be pushed.

Unfortunately, when you're traveling and moving from place to place, you can't predict your film needs. Therefore, you should take a balanced assortment of film along with you. It can be distressing to have a picture possibility before you and not have the right film in your gadget bag.

We carry Kodachrome 64, Agfachrome 64, Ektachrome 200 and 400 (daylight), Ektachrome 160 (tungsten), and Tri-X black-and-white film in our gadget bags at all times.

The Kodachrome and Agfachrome films are for general shooting and account for 90 percent of the pictures.

The Ektachrome 200 and 400 films (daylight) are for dim-light shooting at dusk, for shooting in poor weather, and for night pictures in order to stop the movement of cars and people.

Ektachrome 160 film (tungsten) is for indoor use at shows, theaters, nightclubs, and places where artificial lights are used. We routinely double the ASA of this film, which makes practically all indoor-lighted situations possible without flash.

Tri-X is a good all-purpose film, in case we want to shoot some black-and-white pictures. With careful development, this film gives reproduction-quality enlargements.

On a trip, it's best to use both film and equipment that you have already tested. Don't experiment while you're traveling, because you may not be able to repeat some of the shots.

FILTERS AND HOW TO USE THEM

Some filters help to counteract certain light conditions in a photograph. There are others which can be used for special effects.

Correction Filters
In the first category are the filters that we have listed in the equipment section.

- The UV (ultraviolet absorption) filter to protect your lenses

- The polarizing filter to cut glare and increase contrast

- The 80A filter to correct daylight color emulsion to tungsten lighting

- The 85B filter to correct tungsten film to daylight

- The two filters to correct fluorescent light: an FLD for daylight film and an FLB for tungsten film.

None of these filters alters the color; rather they correct it, so that the picture will appear natural.

Special-Effects Filters

The second category of filters—for special effects—includes so many that a catalog is needed to classify them. These comprise not only the color tint filters, but those for prism effects, split fields, star effects, and many others. You can play around with these filters and they are fun, but you may not have much time on a trip to experiment. It is far better to try these special effects before leaving. Then if some of the filters appeal to you, take them along and use them for certain effects you might want. A star filter, for example, can come in very handy for candlelight-ed scenes.

You can also use some of the filters made for black-and-white correction with color film. When the sky is gray, for example, and you want an orange sunset, you can manufacture one by using an orange or red filter.

The thing to remember about filters is: Don't use one unless you really need to, because filter glass never measures up to lens optics and you will lose some sharpness.

FLASH—WHEN AND HOW TO USE IT

There are times when flash is absolutely necessary; there are other times when it will help; and there are occasions when, unfortunately, it is used but is not needed or is completely useless.

Flash *is necessary* when there is not enough light to shoot by, or when you want to stop action in poor light. But you must remember that each flash unit can throw its light only a certain distance. Beyond that distance your subject will not be illuminated. The flash's carrying power depends on the strength of the unit and the speed (the ASA rating) of the film that you are using. The stronger the light, which usually means the heavier the unit, the farther it will light the scene; and the higher the ASA rating of the film, the more sensitive it is to the light output. So by changing to a faster film, you can get more "light" out of your flash.

It's easy to determine the exposure for your flash shots. You can use the guide number (G.N.) or a flash with an automatic system. The automatic system is easier, because the unit does most of the work. All you have to do is to choose the *f*-stop that falls within the range of the distance you are from the subject, and the unit will measure out the exact light needed when you flash.

The guide-number system takes a little mathematics. First you have to know the G.N. of your unit with the film that you are using, because the G.N. changes with the ASA rating. Then, divide the G.N. by the distance, in feet, that you are from the subject. Finally, set the f-stop to the nearest number corresponding to this result. Following is an example of how this works: If the G.N. for your flash is 80 with Ektachrome 200 or 400 film and you are 10 feet from your subject, then you would divide 80 by 10, with a result of 8. The 8 would then be converted to f/8 as the setting for your picture.

Whichever system you use, always be sure that your shutter setting is on the *sync* speed for your flash so that you don't get a partially exposed frame.

Flash with Daylight

Flash can be used to help out a daylight scene that is unevenly lighted, such as an indoor-outdoor scene where you want to see the people inside and the view of the outside To take a picture like this, you have to do some calculating.

First set your shutter on *sync* speed for your camera (usually 1/60 sec.). Then take a meter reading of the outside scene through the window and set your f-stop for that. To balance this with the light from your flash, divide the f-stop of your outside reading into the G.N. of your flash. This will give you the distance in feet for correct flash exposure. Take your combination flash-daylight scene from this distance and both your indoor flash scene and your outdoor background will be correctly exposed.

Flash with Indoor Lighting

The color and exposure of interior scenes with indoor lighting can also be helped by the addition of flash. The technique for figuring the exposure is similar to the combination daylight-flash shots.

If you would like to illuminate your subject with flash but would also like to have glowing lamps showing, then shoot at the calculated flash f-stop setting but slow your shutter speed down to 1/15 sec., or for more glow, to 1/8 sec. You should get a good overall flash exposure and the added slow shutter speed will register the lamplight. This makes a very pleasing picture, because the warm glow of the lights adds a natural look.

You can also use flash to correct the color balance of the light when you are using outdoor film *indoors,* so that you don't have to use a filter. To do this, first take a meter reading of the interior. Next, stop down one-half to one stop, depending on the size of the room. When shooting, bounce your flash off the ceiling or a wall. This procedure will correct the color balance of the indoor light on outdoor film, and the additional light from the flash will also give the correct exposure.

When you shoot this combination of flash and existing light, the interior lighting on outdoor color film will be warm but not the blood-red color you normally would get.

It is best to bracket and make additional shots when using both of these techniques so that you have a choice among the results.

When Not to Use Flash

The first and most obvious useless use of flash is when you are sitting in the upper rows of a stadium and expect to take an exposure of the distant scene below with a peanut-size flashbulb or a "lightning-bug" output strobe unit. This cannot be done. Just check the instructions with your unit and you'll see that the light won't reach far enough.

Another time not to flash is when the lighting is strong enough to take pictures by available light. Stage shows, night-club acts, and other illuminated scenes can be photographed with a fast, tungsten film. The resulting photo will be better than a flat flash picture, because it will show the dramatic lighting that makes the scene interesting.

Flash for portraits is unsatisfactory because it produces a harsh flat light that either washes out the features or accentuates the flaws. If you must use flash, it is best to soften the effect by bouncing the flash off the wall or ceiling. For bounced light, open up two stops from normal flash exposure to compensate for the added distance.

Generally, the best policy is not to use flash unless you must.

FOCUSING—GENERAL RULES

If you are in doubt when focusing on a scene and want the whole scene to be in focus, pick an object or person about one third of the distance into the picture and use it as your focus point. This rule of thumb will give you the most depth of field.

Where there is a dominant subject, focus directly on your center of interest and do not worry about the rest of the scene.

Selective Focus

A good way to get rid of bothersome and busy backgrounds is to open your lens to a larger f-stop so that your depth of field is short and the background goes blurry. How much you open the lens depends on the depth of your subject, and the way to judge the effect is to look at the image with the depth-of-field preview button depressed. (If your camera doesn't have one, you'll have to approximate by using your depth-of-field scale. Usually, your calculations do not have to be critically accurate.) If you open up to stops of f/4 or larger, move in close to your subject, and compensate for the larger lens opening by increasing your shutter speed. Your background will disappear into a nice blur.

Blurring out the background is especially effective when taking portraits. Not only will the larger opening give a more pleasing focus on the face (be sure to focus right on the iris of the eye in full-face portraits), but because you are close up to your subject the background will be even more out of focus.

Selective focus is a good technique to use for portrait close-ups. By shooting with a moderate telephoto lens (80 mm to 135 mm) and opening up to apertures of f/2.8 to f/4, you can get the effect of large-format professional portraiture. The longer-focal-length lens and the large lens opening on a 35 mm format will approximate the "sharp eyes and soft-focus look" of the larger cameras and longer-focal-length portrait lenses.

Focusing with the Depth-of-Field Scale

The depth-of-field scale markings on the barrel of your lens show the near and far limits of what is in focus at the different f-stop settings.

These marks are located at the top of your lens. To use them, first focus your lens on the subject. Next, look at the depth-of-field marks for the f-stop you are using, and check these against the distance marks to see how near and how far the zone of sharp focus extends. This will be your *depth of field*. It is useful to know what depth of field you have when photographing moving subjects, or in determining how much of the foreground and the background of a still subject is sharp.

A word on moving subjects. It is impossible to focus accurately on moving subjects. So instead of sharp focusing, you can "guesstimate" the distance by setting your focus between the depth-of-field marks on your lens. This way if the subject moves closer, or farther away, you will still be in focus. This system will only work for normal and wide-angle lenses.

The depth-of-field scale is also useful when you want to shoot a scene with maximum depth of field. This might be a street scene, a scenic with a person or an object in the foreground, or an interior of a long room or a building; in other words, a situation where your subject has depth and where you want everything equally sharp. For such scenes, set the far distance marker for the f-stop you're using on infinity. The near distance marker for that stop will show you where this maximum depth of field begins. This technique is especially effective with wide-angle lenses where your image can be sharp as close as 3 feet and as far as infinity. By doing this you are, in effect, focusing at one-third of the distance into the scene.

Prefocusing for Action

Prefocusing is a way of taking pictures of moving subjects and making sure that they will be sharp.

The method is to focus on a spot that your subject will have to cross, and to shoot the picture when the subject arrives at that spot. This works especially well when taking candids of people walking. Look ahead so that you can see your subject coming; decide how close you want to take the picture; and focus on just about anything on that spot. It can be a crack in the pavement, a curb edge on a street crossing, or a light pole or object that your subject will have to pass.

A shutter speed of 1/125 sec. is sufficient to stop the action of subjects walking toward you, but if they are running, or if the angle is from the side, 1/250 sec. or even 1/500 sec. is safer.

Prefocusing is the system that sports photographers use when covering fast-moving events. In summary, it is preframing the picture area before the action arrives so that you are ready to shoot instantly when your subject steps on the spot.

Casual candids such as this shot of a Parisian sidewalk bookstall can be taken unobtrusively. First focus on your scene and set the exposure. Then hold the camera at your waist, or dangling by the strap around your neck, directed toward the scene. Shoot without raising the camera to eye-level when you see the action you want.

HIP SHOOTING

"Shooting from the hip" is a good technique to use when you want to make candid photographs of people in public places without intruding. The practice gets its name from the sharpshooters of the old-time Wild West shows.

The trick is to preset your camera for an average distance and exposure and, with the camera dangling around your neck, to keep your finger on the shutter release. When you see a situation that you want to photograph, instead of bringing the camera up to your eye, turn your body to aim at the subject, hold steady, and press the button. This system takes a little practice, but it really works — and it's fun. You should use a wide-angle lens if you can because your framing won't be exact and you'll need the additional depth of field that a short focal length gives. Remember that you don't have to be focused exactly. Check the scale on your lens to see how much depth of field you have at the *f*-stop you are using.

Where you focus is important. In this shot of the Tuileries gardens the sharp focus on the colorful balloons draws the eye away from the busy background. There are times when you can make a stronger picture if you focus on something specific and let the rest of your scene be out-of-focus.

INSURANCE

Check with your insurance agent to be sure that all of your cameras, lenses, and accessories are insured for your trip abroad. This is a good time to make certain that your equipment is fully insured at *all* times.

If your home insurance doesn't cover your gear, then take out a camera floater on your present policy. This costs a little more, but may save you a major investment in replacing lost or stolen equipment.

If you have a great deal of equipment, you may have to take out a special policy, since most household insurance plans only cover a minimum, such as one camera with one or two lenses.

INTERIOR SHOOTING

The chief difference between indoor and outdoor picture-taking is that indoors you need more exposure to compensate for the poorer light. Because of this need for a longer exposure, you often have to support your camera. Usually this is best done with a tripod, but when traveling, such a heavy piece of equipment is cumbersome to carry around. (A good substitute is a small tabletop tripod that will fit into your gadget bag, or pocket for that matter.)

Another problem indoors is that sometimes you cannot back up far enough to get your subject into the frame. A wide-angle lens is the solution to this problem. There are several focal lengths to choose from: a 35 mm which is acceptable for most situations, a 28 mm which is usually sufficient, and a 24 mm which will always work. Of course, there are times when a normal 50 mm lens will take in your scene.

Besides supporting your camera and using a wide-angle lens, if the scene is lighted by tungsten light rather than daylight, you must either use a tungsten-balanced film or adapt your daylight film by use of a conversion filter. Ektachrome 160 film (tungsten) works very well in interiors illuminated by light bulbs, spotlights, or even candlelight. You can also use daylight film with an 80A conversion filter.

Some interiors are illuminated by fluorescent lighting. This kind of light produces a sickly green color on any film. To correct this off color, you should use a correction filter like the Tiffen FLD for daylight film or the FLB for tungsten film.

Don't be afraid to take interior shots. Just find a convenient doorway, wall, or column against which you can support your camera and keep it plumb both vertically and horizontally so that your picture is not crooked. (For a description of how to make these supported exposures, see "Tripod and Tripod-less Exposures.")

METRIC CONVERSION INFORMATION

When You Know	Multiply by	To Find
inches (in.)	25.4	millimetres (mm)
feet (ft.)	0.3048	metres (m)
miles (mi.)	1.609	kilometres (km)
ounces (oz.)	28.349	grams (g)
pounds (lbs.)	0.453	kilograms (kg)
pounds per square inch (psi.)	0.0703	kilograms per square centimetre (kg/sqcm)
cubic feet (cu. ft.)	0.0283	cubic meters
Fahrenheit temperature (F)	0.5556 after subtracting 32	Celsius temperature (C)

MUSEUMS

When photography is permitted, museums make great picture-hunting grounds. You can take good slide copies of the paintings you admire in the museums where photography is permitted and you don't have to use a flash or a tripod. You can use a fast daylight color film, such as Ektachrome 200 or 400, which can be shot at the rated film speed, or pushed to a faster ASA. To determine whether to push the film, take an exposure reading of one of the darker paintings. If you can shoot at f/2.8 at 1/30 sec., then you can use the rated ASA. If not, keep doubling the ASA on your meter, or, if you have a through-the-lens meter, the ASA dial of your camera, until you can shoot at the above setting.

You can safely double the ASA of Ektachrome film from 200 to 400 without much loss in film quality. It can be further pushed to 800, but that requires very special handling. The trick is never to push film unless you must; and if you have a good camera technique and a steady hand, you should be able to open up to f/2 and be steady at 1/15 sec.

Remember, if you push a film roll at the beginning, then you have to shoot the entire roll at that ASA; you can't change your mind and start pushing in midroll. (See "Pushing Film.")

When taking the picture, be sure that you are lined up directly in front of the painting and that you are holding the camera level, both horizontally and vertically, or you may not get the whole painting in focus. Remember to turn your camera to the vertical format for vertical pictures so that you will get a full-size image.

If you are not familiar with the artist or the work, take an extra close-up shot of the nameplate as a reminder.

You can also shoot displays, but be careful of the lighting. If a display is spotlighted, use high-speed tungsten film. This can be pushed just like daylight film.

Be sure to mark all pushed rolls of film with the ASA number that you used and advise the lab when you send it in for processing.

In the Louvre museum you will have a chance to copy your favorite works of art. Be sure to line up squarely in front of the work to avoid distortion, and keep your focus sharp.

NIGHT SHOOTING

Night shooting is strictly a matter of time exposures for which a tripod or other support is needed (see "Tripod and Tripod-less Exposures.")

The easiest and best time to take "night" pictures is not at night, but at dusk. This is the time of day when the building outlines can still be seen against the sky, and the bright inside lights as well as the street illumination are turned on. At this time exposure determination is easy; just take a straight meter reading of the scene and shoot. Be sure to use a tripod or some other support for sharpness.

Determining the proper exposure is more difficult at night, because bare-light readings throw the meter off, giving you the exposure for the existing light sources, not the lighted scene itself. To get a correct overall reading, take the metered reading from an illuminated area, not from the light bulb itself; or figure an average between your high and low readings for the correct setting.

No matter how accurately you try to meter night scenes, there will be some discrepancy because of *reciprocity failure*. (This simply means that most film is not made for long exposures; therefore, you can't tell how it is going to behave.) So, rather than get up-tight about your exposures, just bracket (see "Bracketing").

Use daylight color film for illuminated night scenes. It gives a warm cast that offsets the blue haze of night.

If you don't have a meter or can't get a reading from the one you have, bracket on the following exposures: For fully illuminated buildings, on Ektachrome 200 film (daylight), use 1/4 sec. at f/2; and if you are shooting with Kodachrome 64, use 1 sec. at f/2. Since light conditions vary, always bracket.

The interior of the Sainte-Chapelle is a place where you can try pushing the ASA of the film, especially if you're without a tripod, to steady slow exposures. Remember that if you do change the ASA of a film you have to finish the roll at the same increased speed.

PUSHING FILM

There are times when you will want to take pictures in low-light situations where you do not want to, or cannot, use flash. In such cases you can "push" your film by using it at a higher ASA rating than the manufacturer gives. By doing this you under-expose the whole roll of film, then compensate by having it overdeveloped when it is processed.

To push a film, set the ASA dial on your camera or expo-sure meter to a higher number than the one marked on the film box. The best policy is to increase the ASA rating by doubling it—for example, from 160 to 320, or 200 to 400. Each time you double the ASA rating you can shoot at one f-stop smaller (or one shutter speed faster). Hence the term to "push one stop, two stops," etc.

You can "push", or increase the speed, of most films safely up to a two-times increase (200 ASA to 800 ASA). Ektachrome can be pushed, at an added cost for processing. But if you push more than two times you will have difficulty in finding a commer-cial lab to process the film. Not all of them will do it. Kodachrome can be pushed only at a very high cost for processing, and very few labs will handle it. (The Eastman Kodak Company will not accept Kodachrome for push processing.)

When you push film you not only increase the speed but you also change the characteristics. In black-and-white film the grain is increased and there is loss of detail in the highlight and shadow areas. In color film, the grain is increased, blacks are lost, and there is a color shift.

Important. You must remember when you "push" a film that you have to do it for the *whole roll* and you *MUST* mark on the roll how much you increased it so that you can tell the lab how to process it.

Tripodless exposures, such as this interior of the Centre Georges Pompidou, can be made by holding the camera firmly against the top of a rail-ing or the side of a pole. Stead-iness will be increased if you use the self-timer to trip the shutter.

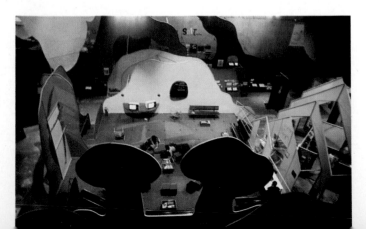

SELF-TIMER USES

The primary use of a self-timer is to include yourself in a picture, but it has other uses too. You can use it to trip the shutter while you are holding the camera against a support during time exposures or when you are shooting with a long telephoto lens. (In most SLR's you can lock up the mirror and release the shutter with the self-timer to avoid vibration.)

The self-timer can also be used to trip the shutter when you want to take an overhead shot of a decorated ceiling. Simply place the camera on the floor, lens up, set the self-timer, and step out of the lens range while the shutter trips.

SHOW SHOOTING

You can take pictures of stage performances, outdoor-lighted spectacles, and even nightclub acts with the existing light.

Use Ektachrome 160 film (tungsten) and double the ASA. You can take a meter reading if there is enough sidelight to see your meter, but if you cannot, here is a guide list of exposures you can use.

- If it is average white-colored stage lighting, you can shoot tungsten film at its normal ASA at 1/30 sec. and f/4.

- If colored gels are used, the exposure can vary down to 1/15 sec. at f/2. (In this case, it is better to double or even triple the rated ASA (to 320 or 640) and shoot at 1/30 sec. at f/2.8 because it's difficult to hold the camera steady at lower shutter speeds, and lower than f/2.8, the depth of field is very shallow.)

A moderate telephoto of 85 mm to 105 mm is ideal for a large image. Don't try to take in all of the stage, unless the scenery is your point of interest, because shooting at slow shutter speeds doesn't really produce very sharp images, and you won't be able to enlarge the image very much.

Watch the action and make your exposures when a movement has just been completed, or when there is no motion. Try to click the shutter when there is a peak in the music, or other stage sound, to cover up the shutter noise.

Show shooting is a matter of practice, since the lighting changes from scene to scene, and even while you are shooting. Until you get the hang of it, and sometimes even after you do, bracket your exposure for safety (see "Bracketing").

TRIPOD AND "TRIPOD-LESS" EXPOSURES

The ideal way to make long exposures is by putting your camera on a sturdy tripod. Unfortunately, sturdy usually means heavy. A full-size tripod is a nuisance on a trip unless you are a real aficionado, or you are taking pictures for money. On the other hand, just because you are using a small camera, you should not make the mistake of using a flimsy, lightweight tripod.

The next best bet to a full-size tripod is a tabletop tripod that you can carry in your gadget bag. Even these have to be sturdy. By sturdy, we mean that when the camera is mounted on it, the tripod doesn't move *at all*. This calls for legs that are widespread enough for balance, with a ball-and-socket joint that locks rigid.

Tripod-less exposures are possible but they take great care. You *must* hold the camera against something, such as a wall, a door frame, a pole, or even a tree trunk, and trip the shutter with a cable release or the self-timer. A self-timer works for exposures up to 1 sec., but you need a cable release for longer exposures on "B" (bulb).

The ideal compromise on a trip is to take a tabletop tripod and use it on top of ledges and tables, and hold it against doorways and trees. The tabletop tripod can also be converted to a chest pod by opening up the legs and resting them on your chest to steady handheld exposures.

Outdoor sidewalk cafés are easy to photograph. For added color, wait for some interesting passerby, such as the uniformed French policemen at this Montmartre café.

WET WEATHER SHOOTING

Often the best time to shoot scenes is right after a rain, because the atmosphere has been washed clean and the dust and dirt are off the foliage. Then, just when the sun is trying to break through, there is a luminous light that gives full color saturation.

It is also a time to look for reflections on the pavement and in the puddles of water.

You can also take pictures *in* the rain, but protect your camera and gadget bag by carrying along a piece of plastic to cover them. An umbrella is essential to keep the rain off the lens. One way to use an umbrella and still keep your hands free is to stick the handle down the back of your neck inside your raincoat or jacket, and wrap the camera strap around the handle, pulling it taut as you take the picture.

Don't let wet weather prevent you from taking pictures. A parade in the rain, or with the sun bursting through the clouds, can add a twist to your sunny-side coverage.

X-RAY EXPOSURE

Although there are a number of bags and containers on the market that are said to protect your films from x-rays at airport security checks, our advice is *do not subject your film to x-ray exposure*. Even if one dose of x-rays won't affect your film, additional exposure every time you have to go through security (particularly when you are making several stops on your trip) might fog your film and cause a loss of quality especially in color material. Our suggestions for traveling with film are:

- do not pack your film in the baggage to be checked into the hold

- keep your film in a separate bag (preferably of clear plastic) that can be examined with ease

- politely ask the security guards to hand-examine your film bag, and, even if they tell you that their machines will not hurt your film, be firm — if necessary ask for a supervisor

- arrive early at the security area, so that you will not be forced to rush through without personal attention

- keep smiling, and thank the guards — remember that they are there for our protection

- film should be removed from the camera because security guards usually insist that metal contraptions be x-rayed or opened for inspection. (See "Changing Film in Midroll" for tips on how to do this.)

127